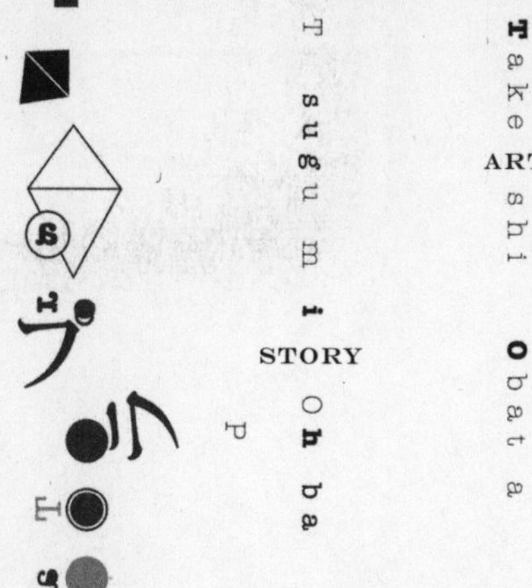

ART Takeshi Obata

STORY Tsugumi Ohba

Platinum End

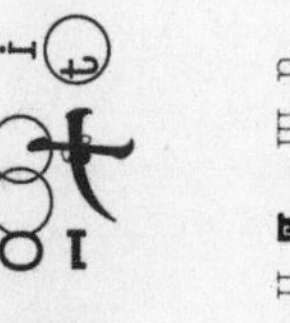

PLATINVM END

3

CONTENTS

3

#7 Death Sentence

HIT ME WITH A RED ARROW. THAT WILL PROVE THAT I'M NOT BEING CON-TROLLED.
I'VE GOT A FIRST-RANK ANGEL, BUT I CAN'T USE MY ARROWS AT THE MOMENT. DON'T WORRY!
FSHHH AAAAAAA
WHY DOES HE SEEM SO DESPERATELY MISERABLE...?

DO IT QUICK.

HFF

WHAT IF I WAS UNDER METRO-POLIMAN'S CONTROL?

HFF

HE'S GOT A POINT.
PIERCE HIM, SAKI.
IT WILL GO THROUGH THE GLASS.

...
FSHHH
HH H-H
...

WHAT ARE YOU WAITING FOR?! DO IT!

WAIT A MOMENT.

?

ARE YOU SURE YOU WANT HIM FALLING IN LOVE WITH SAKI, MIRAI?

IS THIS REALLY THE TIME?!

AND IT'S NOT JUST UP TO MIRAI. THERE'S SAKI'S FEELINGS TO CONSIDER AS WELL.

...

NO! IT'S JUST PROPER SENSE TO USE AN ARROW ON ANY GOD CANDIDATE WHO SHOWS UP!

IF SAKI CAN'T DO IT, THEN IT SHOULD BE YOU, MIRAI!
!

EITHER ONE OF YOU! JUST DO IT!

I DON'T HAVE MUCH TIME!

KWIIIII

I FIGURED I SHOULD THINK VERY HARD BEFORE USING MY ARROWS...

...BUT IN THIS CASE...

NO, I'M SAYING YOU DON'T NEED TO USE ANY ARROWS AT ALL.
!

IN FACT, YOU *SHOULDN'T* HIT HIM WITH ARROWS.

WE SHOULDN'T?
YES.

SHF
I MEAN...

HE'S NOT LYING.

RIGHT?

...

FSHHHHHHHHHHH

SHF
...
SHF
THANKS.
IF NASSE SAYS YOU'RE NOT LYING, THEN IT'S BOUND TO BE TRUE.

IN FACT, YOU HAVE NOTHING TO GAIN BY TELLING SOMEONE TO HIT YOU WITH AN ARROW.
NORMALLY IT WOULD BE YOU TRYING TO HIT US.
SO NATURALLY, WE WANTED TO GET YOU FIRST...

BUT IF WE'RE GOING TO JOIN FORCES, THEN AS NASSE SAYS, IT'S BETTER NOT TO PIERCE YOU.

IF YOU'RE PIERCED, YOU WILL FOLLOW THE ORDERS OF THE PIERCER...

...BUT YOU WILL NOT SPEAK YOUR OWN MIND, ONLY THE THINGS THAT MATCH UP WITH OUR POINT OF VIEW.

...

...

I TRUST YOU.
SHF

ME TOO ...
FFT

YOU'RE NOT GOING TO PIERCE ME...
I SEE ...

THEN LET'S CONTINUE.
SEE, I DON'T HAVE MUCH TIME...

WHEN YOU SAY...
...YOU DON'T HAVE MUCH TIME...

YEAH ...
WHAT I MEAN IS...

...

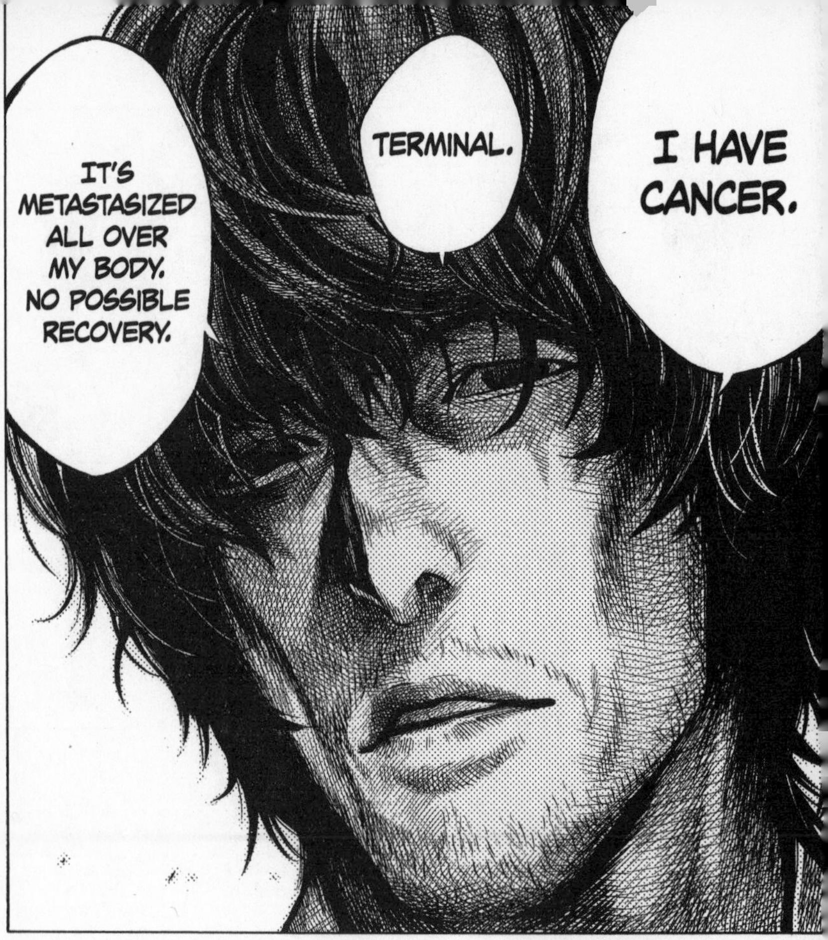

I HAVE CANCER.

TERMINAL.

IT'S METASTASIZED ALL OVER MY BODY. NO POSSIBLE RECOVERY.

DON'T LOOK AT ME LIKE THAT.
FOUR MONTHS AGO, I WAS GIVEN THREE MONTHS TO LIVE...
AND RIGHT ABOUT THREE MONTHS AFTER THAT SENTENCE, AN ANGEL CAME TO ME.
I WAS 100 PERCENT CONVINCED IT WAS MY ESCORT TO THE AFTERLIFE.
HUH? YOU'RE NOT?
NO.

I SEE.
SO I'M NOT DEAD YET...
I SEE...
...
NANATO MUKAIDO.

YOU HAVE LOST YOUR HOPE IN LIFE.
HOPE? DON'T BE STUPID.
I'M GOING TO DIE IN MOMENTS.
I HAVE NO LIFE LEFT TO HOPE FOR.

I LIVED MY LIFE AS BEST I COULD, I THINK...
IT'S AN EARLY END, BUT THERE'S NOTHING I CAN DO... IT WAS MOSTLY WORTHWHILE.
EVERY HUMAN BEING HAS TO DIE...
IT'S JUST ONE LESS PUNY LITTLE MAN IN THE WORLD, LOOKING FORWARD TO THAT LAST SMOKE BEFORE HE DIES.
IS THAT SO? BUT...
I READ IN AN OLD BOOK THAT "THOSE WHO ACCEPT DEATH WHEN THEIR ABILITY TO LIVE IS DENIED THEM CAN BECOME STRONGER THAN THOSE WHO SIMPLY LOSE THEIR HOPE IN LIFE."
STRONGER? WHAT DO YOU MEAN?

IT IS A STORY THAT MIGHT CONVINCE YOU THAT LIFE IS WORTHWHILE AGAIN.
IF YOU CAN BECOME GOD BEFORE GIVING IN TO DISEASE...
...THEN YOU WILL OVERCOME IT, AND CAN END UP LIVING FOR THOUSANDS OF YEARS LONGER.

...

I THOUGHT... I WOULD BE LEAVING THEM HELP-LESS...

MY WIFE... OUR CHILD...

THE SECOND ONE ON ITS WAY...

WITH 28 YEARS LEFT ON OUR MORTGAGE ...

OHHH...

MAKE ME A GOD!!
I JUMPED AT THE CHANCE...

BUT IT WASN'T AS EASY AS IT SOUNDED...

THE PROCESS CAN LAST UP TO 999 DAYS... AND IS CHOSEN FROM A FIELD OF 13...
AND NOW YOU HAVE THIS NUTJOB NAMED METROPOLIMAN RUNNING AROUND...

IT'S OBVIOUSLY NOT GOING TO WRAP UP WHILE I'M STILL ALIVE.
SO I DECIDED ...

...TO STOP WASTING MY TIME WITH LIFE-PROLONGING TREATMENT.

FORGET WAITING FOR DEATH IN MY BED. I'D RATHER USE MY WINGS AND ARROWS WHILE I'M STILL ALIVE!
SO I MADE UP MY MIND.

I RESEARCHED THE RICHEST PEOPLE IN JAPAN-- I WON'T SAY WHOM-- AND USING MY RED ARROWS, GOT 200 MILLION YEN IN CASH.

THAT WILL BE FOR MY WIFE AND CHILDREN AFTER I'M GONE...

IT MEANS THEY'LL BE FINE, NO MATTER WHAT HAPPENS.

...

I'M A THIEF. I DON'T DESERVE TO BE GOD.

HOW CAN SOMEONE WHO ONLY THINKS OF HIS OWN NEEDS FIT THAT POSITION?

THAT'S NOT TRUE AT ALL.

YOU DID IT FOR YOUR WIFE AND CHILDREN. THAT'S THE BEST POSSIBLE USE FOR YOUR WINGS AND ARROWS.

I AGREE...

YOU'RE WISHING FOR THE HAPPINESS OF YOUR FAMILY.

HAH...

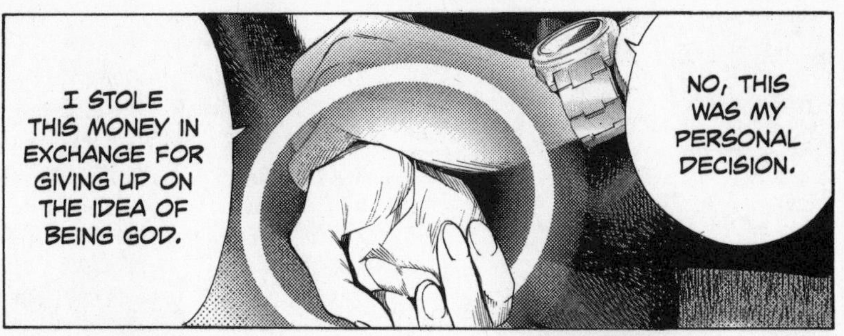
NO, THIS WAS MY PERSONAL DECISION.
I STOLE THIS MONEY IN EXCHANGE FOR GIVING UP ON THE IDEA OF BEING GOD.

I REALLY COULD DIE AT ANY MOMENT NOW.
I TRIED TO THINK ABOUT WHAT I CAN DO WHILE I'M STILL ALIVE...

WHAT CAN I DO TO ENSURE MY CHILDREN'S HAPPINESS?

AT THE VERY LEAST...
...I HAVE TO MAKE SURE THAT METROPOLIMAN DOES NOT BECOME GOD.

IN ORDER TO DO THAT, I MUST MEET AS MANY CANDIDATES AS I CAN WHILE I STILL LIVE...

...AND TEAM UP WITH THEM TO DEFEAT METROPOLIMAN.

IF POSSIBLE, I'D LIKE TO MEET *ALL* OF THEM, SO I CAN SEE FOR MYSELF WHO IS BEST SUITED TO BE GOD.

JUST AS I WAS GETTING THAT IDEA, METROPOLIMAN SUMMONED US TO THE STADIUM.
LET THE 12 OF US MEET AND TALK THINGS OUT!
THE LOCATION... JINBO STADIUM.

I WAS CERTAIN THAT OTHER GOD CANDIDATES WOULD COME... SO I PIERCED 14 DETECTIVES AND PSYCHOLOGISTS— THAT BEING THE UPPER LIMIT OF RED ARROWS I CAN DEPLOY...
...AND SENT THEM ALL INTO THE STADIUM.
AND WE FOUND ...
...THAT YOU TWO WERE CLEARLY SHOWING SIGNS THAT YOU COULD SEE THE ANGELS AND ARROWS...
!

...

I MAY BE LOWER THAN SCUM ...

...BUT NOW THAT I DON'T CARE ABOUT MYSELF, I'VE GAINED CLEARER JUDGMENT OF OTHERS.

WHEN I SAW THE FOOTAGE OF YOU THE DETECTIVES SENT ME, I THOUGHT...

..."THEY LOOK LIKE GOOD PEOPLE."
...

THIS IS BAD NEWS.
?

I WAS EASILY ABLE TO IDENTIFY MIRAI AS A CANDIDATE UPON OUR FIRST MEETING.
AND DESPITE ALL OF OUR WARNINGS AND CAUTION, HE IDENTIFIED YOU AS CANDIDATES AT THE STADIUM.
IT SEEMS THAT THIS TURNED OUT TO OUR BENEFIT IN THIS CASE...
...BUT IT COULD EASILY HAVE SPIRALED OUT OF OUR CONTROL...
...
AND WHAT ABOUT YOU TWO?

DO YOU REALLY FEEL LIKE BEING GOD?

OKAY, OKAY, THAT'S GOOD.
ANY HUMAN BEING WHO *WANTS* TO BE GOD ISN'T RIGHT IN THE HEAD.
...

ALSO, I FOUND ONE OTHER CANDIDATE AT THE BALLPARK.

YOU DID?!

THEY FLEW AWAY, SO I DON'T KNOW WHO IT WAS...

BUT THE KID LOOKED LIKE THIS.
!

THIS PICTURE IS ALL THE EVIDENCE I HAVE TO GO ON FOR NOW.
LET'S WORK TOGETHER AND FIND THIS KID.
...

YES, WE OUGHT TO DO THAT.
RIGHT.

I HAVE A CONDITION YOU MUST MEET FOR MY COOPERATION.
?

PLEASE CONTINUE YOUR TREAT-MENT.
DO NOT GIVE UP ON LIFE.

...

NO. I'VE ALREADY PASSED THE POINT WHERE I SHOULD HAVE DIED...
IT'S YOUR OWN EGO THAT'S SAYING IT'S OKAY TO DIE.

PLEASE THINK ABOUT THE REST OF YOUR FAMILY TOO...

KAKE-
HASHI
...

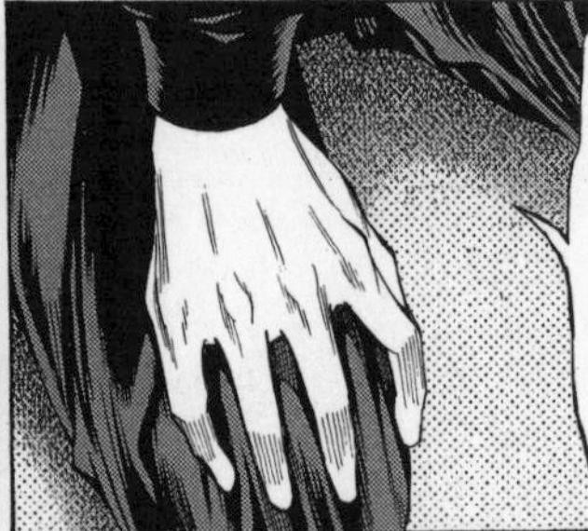
TRY YOUR VERY BEST TO GET TREATMENT, TO SURVIVE AS LONG AS POSSIBLE, FOR YOUR FAMILY'S SAKE.

THAT'S MY CONDITION IF YOU WANT TO RECEIVE MY HELP.

WHY WOULD HE SAY THAT TO A DYING MAN?
ANY TIME SPENT ON TREATMENT IS WASTED...

YEAH... FINE...
I WANT TO LIVE FOR AS MANY DAYS AS POSSIBLE, IT'S TRUE.

GREAT ...

OH, I NEARLY FORGOT. MY NAME'S NANATO MUKAIDO.
I WAS IN CHARGE OF PLANNING NEW PRODUCTS FOR AN APPAREL COMPANY-- UNTIL I HAD TO LEAVE, THAT IS.

KINNG

TKINNG

KI-KINNG

HOW SHOULD I USE THESE THREE SETS OF WINGS AND ARROWS?

YOU CAN'T KILL SOMEONE WITH THE RED ARROWS JUST BY TELLING THEM TO DIE.
AND THEY WON'T KILL ANYONE ELSE IF YOU ORDER THEM TO COMMIT MURDER.
MEANING THERE'S NO WAY TO USE THEM TO CAUSE DEATH WITHOUT HAVING THE WHITE ARROWS LIKE ME.
BUT WHAT IF IT'S A PERSON WHO ALREADY WANTS TO DIE?
SOMEONE WHO'S READY...
Heh...

WHAT?! YOU'RE A SPECIAL RANK WITH WHITE ARROWS?!

DON'T SHOUT LIKE THAT, MR. MUKAIDO.

THOSE WILL COME IN VERY HANDY IN A BATTLE!

WHITE ARROWS... THAT'S GREAT...

...

?

...
SO... HANAKAGO'S ANGEL REVEL IS A SECOND RANK WITH JUST RED ARROWS.

IF I DIE FIRST, PLEASE TAKE MY WINGS AND USE THEM FOR YOURSELF.
Ha ha ...

SMIRK

I TOLD YOU, DON'T TALK ABOUT DYING...
RIGHT, RIGHT, SORRY.

MY ANGEL'S NAME IS BARET.
SHE'S KNOWN FOR BEING THE ANGEL OF KNOWLEDGE, AND WAS A SPECIAL-RANK ANGEL AT ONE POINT.

BARET?
YOU DON'T KNOW HER?

SHE WAS DEMOTED FROM SPECIAL RANK TO FIRST RANK FOR BEING A KNOW-IT-ALL.
ANGELS, GODS... SHE HAS ALL KINDS OF HEAVENLY KNOWLEDGE GLEANED FROM HISTORY.
SHE IS INDEED VERY LEARNED, BUT NOT WITHOUT FLAWS...

I SEE. I'M GETTING THE FEELING THIS MIGHT ACTUALLY WORK.
I'M GOING TO BORROW YOUR TABLE AND TRY TO SUM UP EVERYTHING WE KNOW.
SHWP
KAKEHASHI'S ANGEL, NASSE, IS SPECIAL RANK.
Nass
Mirai Kakehashi

OH! BASED ON WHAT METROPOLIMAN SAID ABOUT HIS ANGEL...
MY ANGEL HAS YOU BEAT FOR SEX APPEAL.
...I'M PRETTY SURE IT'S MEYZA.
MEYZA?

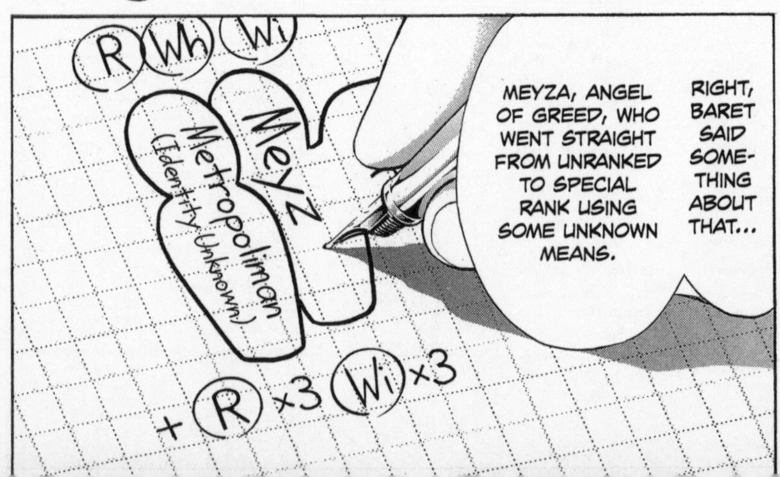
RIGHT, BARET SAID SOMETHING ABOUT THAT...
MEYZA, ANGEL OF GREED, WHO WENT STRAIGHT FROM UNRANKED TO SPECIAL RANK USING SOME UNKNOWN MEANS.
R Wh Wi
Meyz
Metropoliman (Identity Unknown)
+ R x3 Wi x3

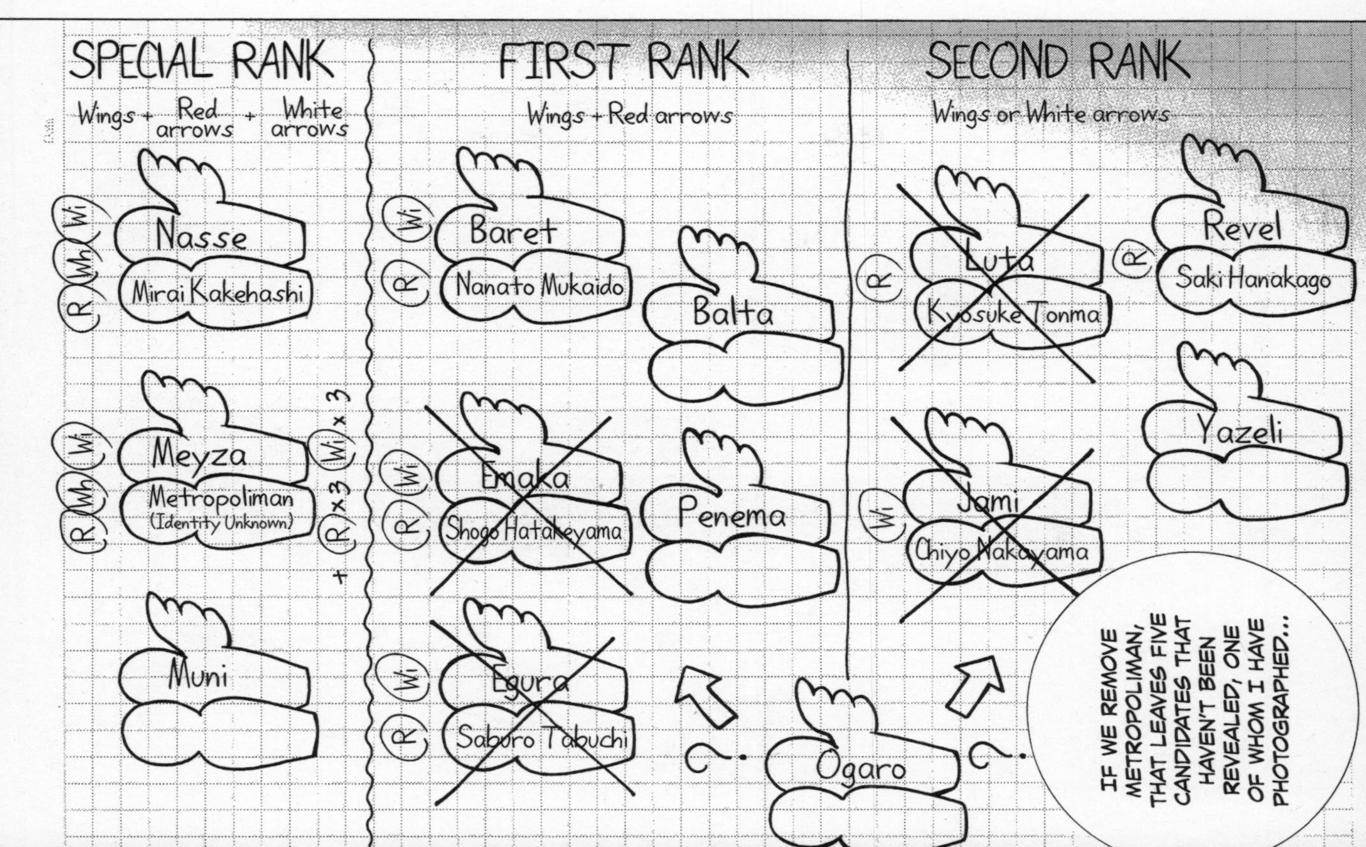
SPECIAL RANK
Wings + Red arrows + White arrows
R Wh Wi
Nasse
Mirai Kakehashi
R Wh Wi
Meyza
Metropoliman (Identity Unknown)
+ R x3 Wi x3
Muni
FIRST RANK
Wings + Red arrows
R Wi
Baret
Nanato Mukaido
Balta
R Wi
Emaka
Shogo Hatakeyama
Penema
R Wi
Egura
Saburo Tabuchi
Ogaro
SECOND RANK
Wings or White arrows
R
Luta
Kyosuke Tonma
R
Revel
Saki Hanakago
Yazeli
Wi
Jami
Chiyo Nakayama
IF WE REMOVE METROPOLIMAN, THAT LEAVES FIVE CANDIDATES THAT HAVEN'T BEEN REVEALED, ONE OF WHOM I HAVE PHOTOGRAPHED...

THAT'S WHAT WE'VE GOT FOR NOW.
KTUNK

PHEW.

OH... THERE'S ONE OTHER THING I WANT US TO HAVE STRAIGHT.

IN THE FUTURE...
...DEPENDING ON WHAT WE DO, YOU MIGHT NEED TO COVER YOURSELVES UP IN PUBLIC.
THE WAY METRO-POLIMAN DOES.

IF WE *ARE* ABLE TO GET FIVE OR SIX OF US TOGETHER, YOU'LL WANT SOME COOL COSTUMES.
IF IT COMES TO THAT, I'M YOUR MAN.

TRUST ME, I DESIGNED OUTFITS FOR A CLOTHING COMPANY. I KNOW WHAT I'M DOING.
UMF

JUST... THINK ABOUT IT.
...
...
KSHNK
SEE YOU TOMOR-ROW.
IF I'M NOT HERE WHEN YOU GET BACK FROM SCHOOL...
...YOU CAN ASSUME I'VE FINALLY DIED.
Ha ha ...

I TOLD YOU NOT TO SAY THAT STUFF!
HA HA, JUST KIDDING!
BYE.

SHWIP
HE WAS... STRANGE.
YES. BUT POSSIBLY VERY HELPFUL.

AFTER ALL, THOSE READY TO DIE ARE VERY STRONG INSIDE.
...

JOSO ACADEMY

DING DONG

SKRITCH

SKRITCH

THAT'S ALL FOR TODAY, CLASS.

STAND!
KTHUNK
FLIP
KTHUNK
BOW!
If I Become God
Kanade Uryu
UNTIL TOMORROW.

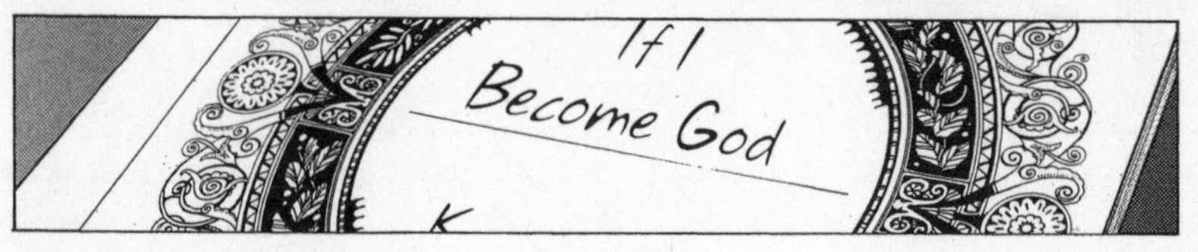
If I Become God

KANADE.

HMM?

C'MON, WILL YOU TAKE ME TO OBSERVE CLUB PRACTICE AGAIN?
YOU REALLY LIKE THAT, DON'T YOU? WELL... I DO TOO.
LET'S VISIT THE MIDDLE SCHOOL CLUB THIS TIME.
YESSS! ♡
MUST BE NICE TO BE THE HEADMASTER'S GRANDSON. YOU CAN GO ANYWHERE YOU WANT.

I CAN'T GET ENOUGH OF SAYURI. AND SHE'S THREE YEARS YOUNGER THAN ME...
GIRLS THAT AGE ARE AT THEIR MOST BEAUTIFUL. THEY'RE SO PURE.

I WISH I COULD GO OUT WITH A GIRL LIKE HER.

IF YOU WOULD DIE TO DO IT WITH HER, I CAN MAKE HER FALL IN LOVE WITH YOU.
SHWP
REALLY?!

BUT THE PART ABOUT DYING IS A 100 PERCENT GUARANTEE.

...

...
I THINK I'LL PASS.

MINAMI-KAWA.
WHAT?
IF YOU COULD HAVE ONE WISH, ANY WISH, WHAT WOULD IT BE?
?!
IF I COULD HAVE ONE THING I REALLY WANTED?
YES.
MONEY. I *REALLY* WANT TO BE RICH.
NOT THAT.

ZWIP
DOESN'T COUNT?
NO.

IT'S TOO SMALL, TOO PERSONAL... I MEAN SOMETHING THAT AFFECTS THE ENTIRE WORLD.

YOU MEAN... LIKE RIDDING THE WORLD OF NUCLEAR POWER AND NUCLEAR WEAPONS?
YEAH, I LIKE THAT.

THEN I WANT ALL UGLY WOMEN TO DISAPPEAR FROM THE WORLD.

...

YOU KNOW WHAT? I'LL ACCEPT THAT.
YEAAAH!

AND THEN I WANT EVERY GUY MORE HANDSOME THAN ME GONE TOO.

WHAT DO *YOU* WANT THEN, KANADE?

...

ME? LET'S SEE...

FSH

IF IT WASN'T SOMETHING REALISTIC, LIKE MAKING PEOPLE DIE...

IF IT WAS SOMETHING TOTALLY IMPOSSIBLE UNLESS ANY WISH COULD COME TRUE...

FSH

I WOULD BRING THE DEAD BACK TO LIFE.

YOUR LITTLE SISTER?

HUH? THEY ALL LEFT.
LET'S GO.

NO... WAIT A SECOND.

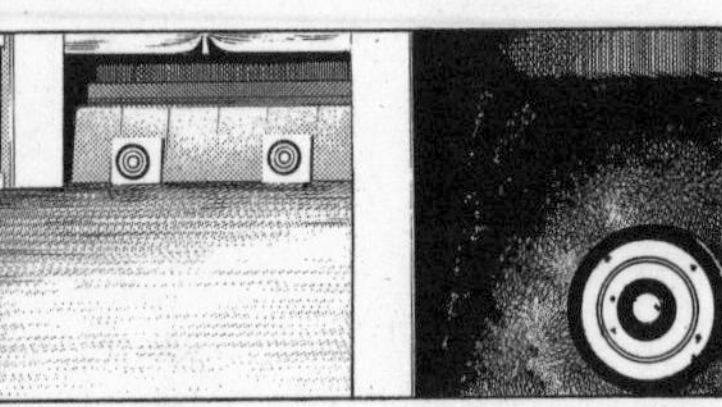

?
DID YOU KNOW THAT IN ARCHERY, THERE'S A SHORT-RANGE TARGET AT 28 METERS, AND A LONG-RANGE TARGET AT 60?

TAP
TAP
TAP

I KNOW 28 METERS IS A SNAP.
BUT 60 METERS...
WHUP
...
SHH...

KW ING---
KI- KW II
TI NG
VSH---

?
WHATCHA DOING?

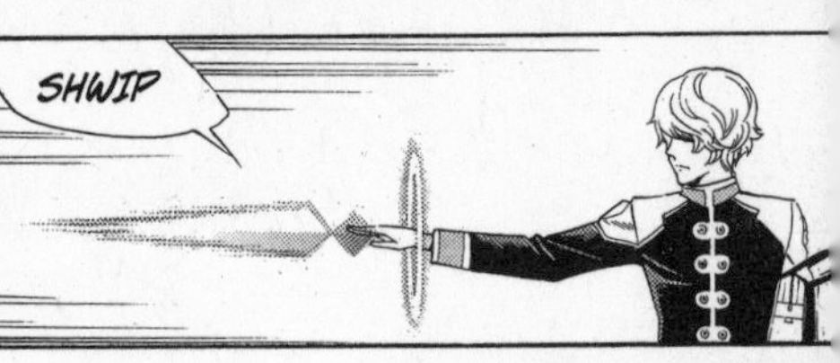
SHWIP

OKAY. LET'S GO.
?

I SEE... IF I CONNECT TWO ARROWS, 60 METERS IS EASY.
WITH THREE, I COULD GET OVER 90 METERS...

WHUP
WHUP
SHA

TAK
WELCOME BACK.
TAK

TAK

TAK
TAK

BEEP

SH

HH

TAK
TAK
TAK
TAK
BEEP
BEEP
BEEP
TAK
VMMMM

HAPPY BIRTHDAY ...

WE'LL SEARCH FOR THIS KID FIRST.
WE HAVE TO COMB OVER THE PAPERS, TV, ONLINE NEWS-- ANYTHING WE CAN FIND.
ANYONE WHO GOT RICH QUICK OR SUDDENLY GOT POPULAR ...
ANY ATHLETE IN A SPEED-BASED SPORT MAKING HUGE GAINS...
BE WARY OF ANYONE FITTING THESE CONDITIONS.
WITH MR. MUKAIDO AROUND, HE MAKES IT VERY CLEAR WHAT WE OUGHT TO BE DOING...
THAT'S THE BENEFIT OF AN ADULT.
BING-BONG
NHT News Alert
A NEWS ALERT!

NHT News Alert

Girl A, killer of multiple middle school students, has escaped from juvenile detention center.

THE GIRL WHO KILLED THOSE THREE FEMALE MIDDLE SCHOOL STUDENTS TWO YEARS AGO?!

WE NOW HAVE AN UPDATE ON GIRL A, THE ESCAPEE IN QUESTION.
AUTHORITIES HAVE RELEASED A NOTE THAT APPEARS TO BE A CRIMINAL DECLARATION.

I already killed three cute little girls
but once I'm free from this place I think I'll be killing more of the ugly ones this time

NHT News Alert

Girl A, killer of multiple middle school students

WHA... WHAT IS THIS?
THIS IS WAY TOO UNNATURAL TO BE ANYTHING ELSE!

...
IF SHE'S UNDER METRO-POLIMAN'S CONTROL, AND HAS HIS WINGS AND RED ARROWS...

ALL THREE OF THOSE MURDERS WERE DONE WITH A KNIFE, RIGHT?

RIGHT. SHE WON'T NEED A WHITE ARROW IF SHE HAS A KNIFE.

AND WITH WINGS, SHE WON'T HAVE ANY TROUBLE ABDUCTING PEOPLE AND STAYING AWAY FROM THE POLICE.

...

LOOKS LIKE WE'RE GOING TO NEED THOSE COSTUMES SOONER THAN I THOUGHT.

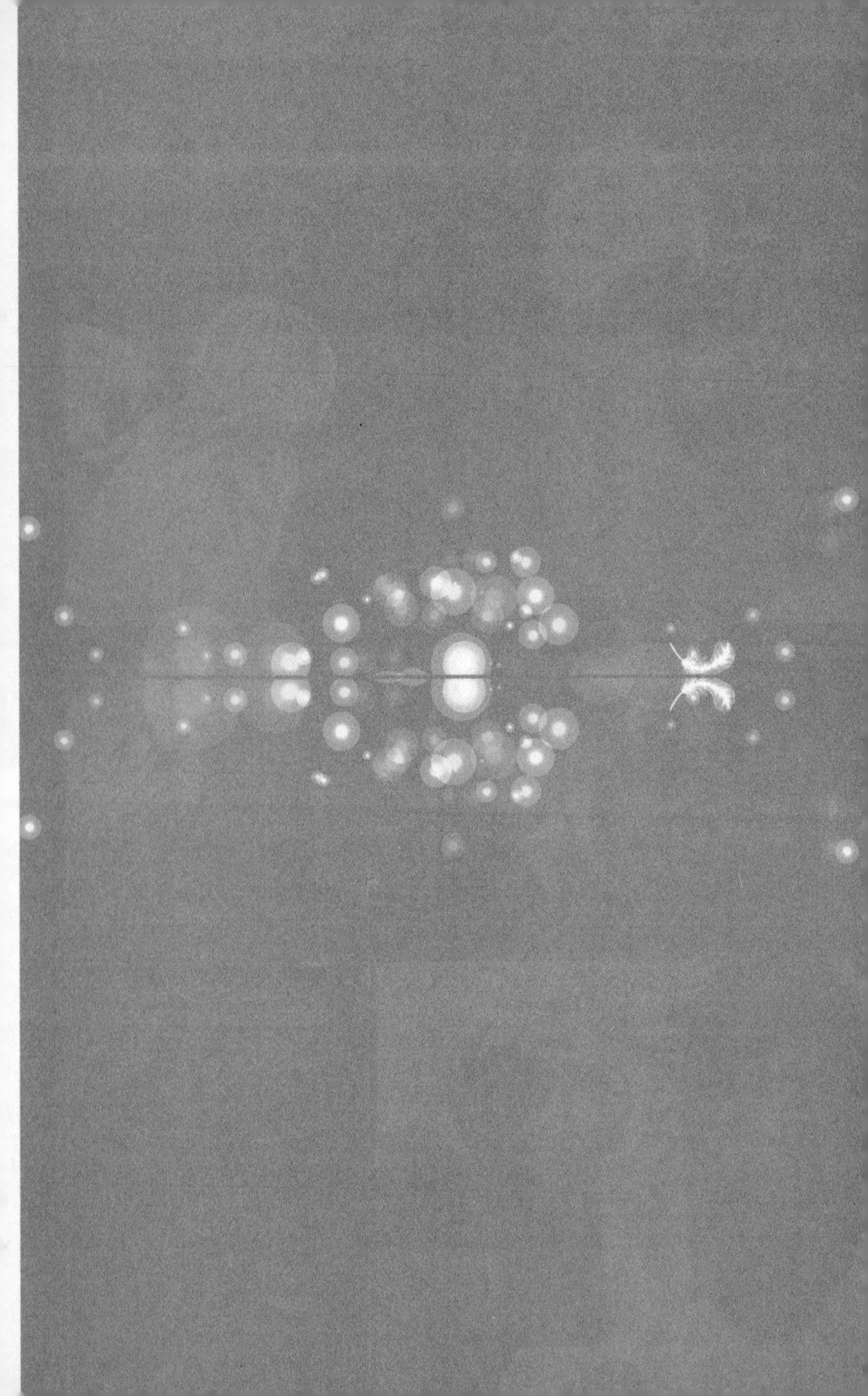

#8 Two Painful Options

GRAH!
KAW!
GAHH!
WHOOOSH
GRAHH!
GRAH
GRAH
GRAH!
GAAAH!

CRAZY!

CRAZY!

THIS IS AWESOME.

AH!

MMM...

AHHH... THIS IS BLISS.
SAME FOR ME.

WHUP
SH
WHUP
HZZ
THIS IS CRAZY.
THIS IS SO CRAZY.
SHE'S NOT *SERIAL KILLER GIRL A* FOR NOTHING. ALREADY ON TO THE NEXT VICTIM.

KCHAK

HUFF !!

HUFF !!

AT LEAST LOCK THE DOOR.
ALSO, YOU'RE BEING REALLY LOUD.
THUMP

OOOO! METRO-POLIMAN! ♡

TMP
♪

YOU CAME! I'M SO HAPPY!
SQUEEN!
WHAT? WHO'S THIS, MISURIN?

I HATE BOYS--THEY'RE ALL SO FILTHY. MASTER POLIMAN'S THE ONLY ONE I LOVE.
RIGHT?

I WAS JUST CHECKING YOUR WORK. SHE WAS TOO BEAUTIFUL! UGLY ONES, I TOLD YOU.
WHAT? MISURIN MADE A MISTAKERIN?
BUT SHE WAS AS FAR DOWN AS I COULD GO!
...

THIS ONE'S TOEING THE LINE TOO.

?

...

FINE. JUST DO AS YOU'RE TOLD.

YES, MASTER POLIMAN! ♡

FWOSH

SHHP

AWW, LEAVING ALREADY?

WE COULD DO A THREE-SOME.

NOT INTER-ESTED.

AWWW, HE LEFT.
HUH? I HAVE NO IDEA WHAT HE LOOKS LIKE.
EVEN THE POLICE WANT TO KNOW.
I'M SURE HE MUST BE VERY HANDSOME INSIDE THERE.
BUT YOU'RE THE ONLY ONE I WANT, MISURIN.
WHAT?!
ISN'T THAT KINDA CRAZY?
EXACTLY. IT'S SUPER CRAZY. I LOVE CRAZY AND DANGEROUS THINGS.
SO LET'S TRY OUT SOMETHING EVEN CRAZIER.
EEK! ♡

HERE, PUT ON THIS BLINDFOLD.
I'LL TIE YOUR HANDS BEHIND YOU.
TUG
HUH?
HUFF!!
OOH, WOW, THIS IS FUN! ♡
HUFF!!
SHH
AND NOW...
SHKK
I'LL USE THIS...

but once I'm free from this place I think I'll be killing more of the ugly ones this time♡

NHT News Alert

Girl A, killer of multiple middle school students, has escaped from a juvenile detention center.

GIRL A'S NAME AND PICTURE WERE LEAKED ONTO THE INTERNET TWO YEARS AGO, RIGHT?

IT'S AN UNFORTUNATE AGE WE LIVE IN...

BUT IT'S TO OUR BENEFIT TO BE ABLE TO RECOGNIZE HER.
THAT'S TRUE.

nile

This is the serial killer of middle school girls!! Mi³

Name: Mimimi Yamada (age 14 in picture) Alias: Mi³ (Misurin)

The insane killer who's captivating the nation

DURING QUESTIONING BY THE POLICE, SHE SAID, "I WANTED TO KILL PEOPLE," "IT WAS THRILLING WHEN I KILLED THEM" AND "I STILL WANT TO KILL MORE." THIS IS HORRIFYING...

THE NET'S BEEN IN A PANIC SINCE THE NEWS OF HER ESCAPE.

IT SAYS SAKURA TV'S TALKING WITH A WITNESS RIGHT NOW.
HUH?!

Girl A, killer of multiple middle school students,
has escaped from a juvenile detention center.
BEEP!

NHT News Alert
Girl A, killer of multiple middle school students,
has escaped from a juvenile detention center.

YES, A STAFF MEMBER OF THE DETENTION CENTER RELEASED HER.
SO YOU'RE SAYING THAT THE STAFF MEMBER HELPED HER ESCAPE ...?
THAT'S RIGHT.

IT WASN'T EVEN AN "ESCAPE," BLEEP WAS SENT OFF WEARING A UNIFORM.
THAT'S RIGHT, WAVING HER HAND AND EVERY-THING.

THIS IS HARD TO BELIEVE... SO WHERE DID GIRL A GO?
WELL... THIS IS THE PART THAT'S TRULY HARD TO BELIEVE.

!
HUH?!
SHE JUST VANISHED.

SIGH...

BZT...

...

METROPOLIMAN COULD HAVE PIERCED THE STAFFER FIRST, BUT HE LIKELY GAVE HER ARROWS AS WELL.

SHE'S GOT RED ARROWS AND WINGS.

FOR WHAT PURPOSE?
PROBABLY TO USE *GIRL A* TO LURE OUT MORE GOD CANDIDATES.
I AGREE ...
METRO-POLIMAN IS ONLY INTER-ESTED IN ELIMINATING RIVALS.

HE GIVES A SERIAL KILLER OBSESSED WITH YOUNG TEEN GIRLS SOME WINGS AND RED ARROWS...
SHE'LL HAVE A VERY EASY TIME KILLING IF SHE SEDUCES HER VICTIMS. IT COULD BE HAPPENING RIGHT NOW...
...

THAT POSSIBILITY WILL SPUR INTEREST IN FINDING AND STOPPING HER...
ESPECIALLY IF IT HAPPENS JUST AFTER WE ALL WITNESSED A LITTLE GIRL'S MURDER AT THE BASEBALL STADIUM.

SO...

THE QUESTION IS, WHAT DO *WE* DO?

UM... DO?

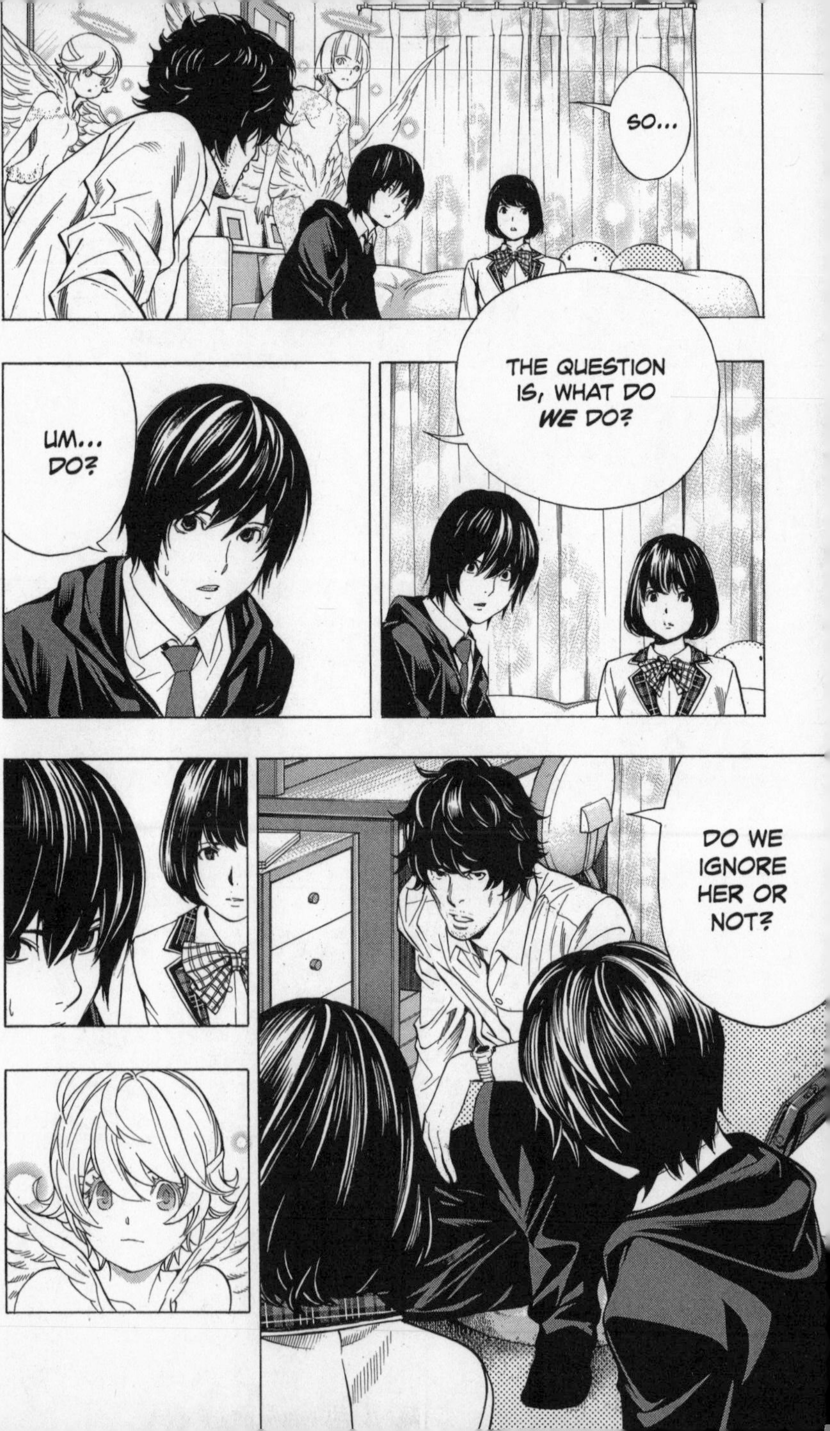

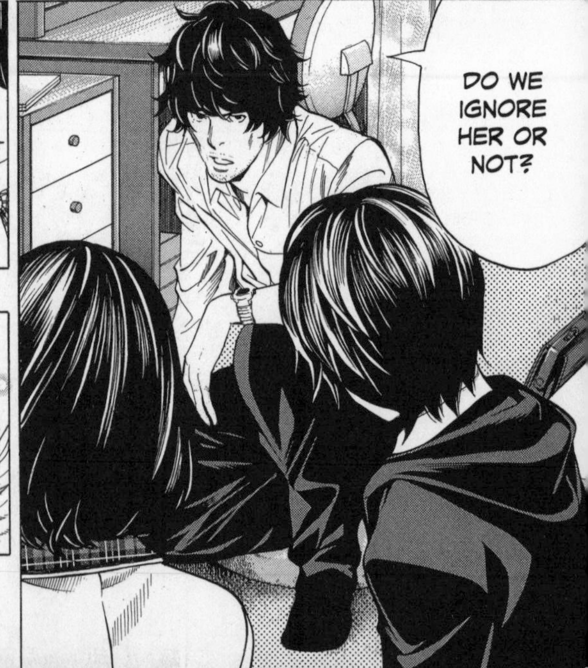
DO WE IGNORE HER OR NOT?

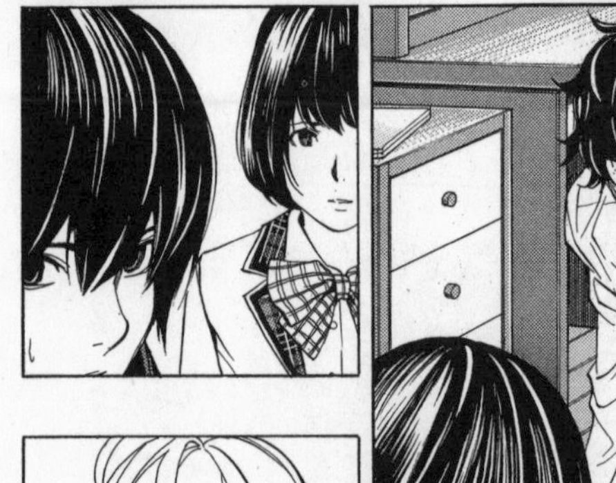

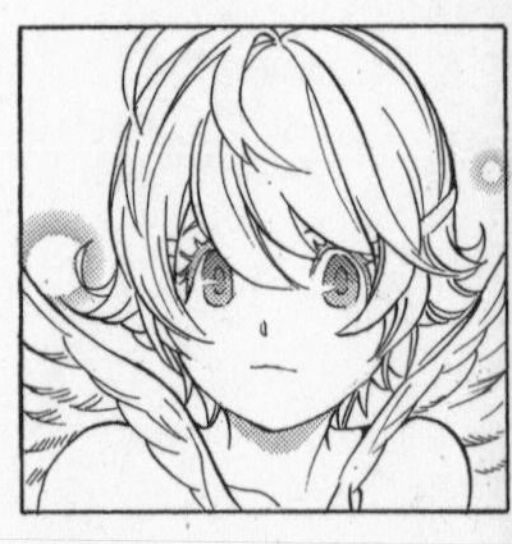

IN 33 DAYS, THE WINGS AND ARROWS THAT METROPOLIMAN GAVE *GIRL A* AFTER HITTING HER WITH HIS OWN RED ARROW WILL DISAPPEAR.

THE POLICE WILL BE ABLE TO CAPTURE HER AFTER THAT, BUT SHE'LL HAVE THE OPPORTUNITY TO KILL ANYONE SHE WANTS, UP TO A MAX OF 14.

YOU'RE ASKING US IF WE'RE GOING TO TAKE METRO-POLIMAN'S BAIT OR NOT?

THAT'S EXACTLY WHAT THIS IS.

...

WHAT DO YOU THINK WE SHOULD DO, MR. MUKAIDO?
ME? I THINK ...

WE SHOULD FIND HER...

... AND KILL HER.

I THINK THAT WHEN METROPOLIMAN COMES TO KILL US AS WE APPROACH *GIRL A*... USING OUR OWN WHITE ARROWS TO KILL HIM...
...IS THE BEST PLAN.
I AGREE.

...
USE WHITE ARROWS...
...TO KILL HIM...

I'M THE ONLY ONE OF US WITH WHITE ARROWS.

...

IF WE KILL METROPOLIMAN, *GIRL A* BECOMES AN ORDINARY GIRL AGAIN AND CAN BE HANDLED APPROPRIATELY.

THE SAME THING APPLIED TO METRO PINK AND GREEN.

YES. METROPOLIMAN IS THE ROOT OF EVERYTHING. IT WILL NOT END UNTIL WE KILL HIM.

CLEARLY THERE'S NO LEVEL TO WHICH HE WON'T SINK, AS HE'S GIVING A SERIAL KILLER WINGS AND ARROWS.
WHAT DO YOU THINK?
PERSONALLY... I WANT TO MAKE SURE I SEE HIM DIE BEFORE I FINALLY KICK THE BUCKET.

...

YOU DON'T AGREE, KAKE-HASHI?

...
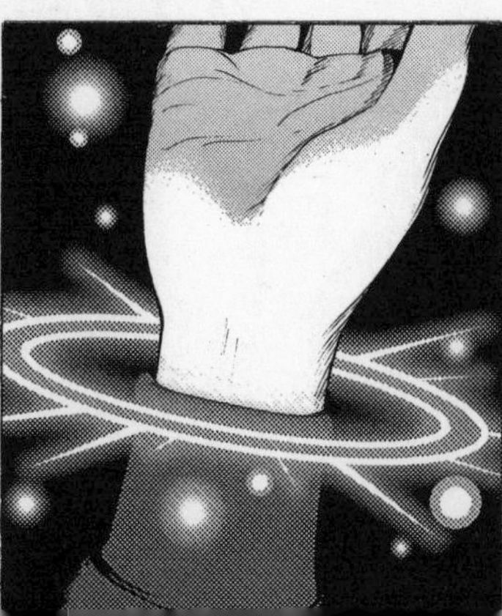

I DON'T WANT TO KILL ANYONE.

WELL, THAT WOULD BE THE PROPER CHOICE.
BUT IN THIS CASE, THINK OF IT AS SELF-DEFENSE. IN MY OPINION, WE SHOULD KILL HIM BEFORE HE KILLS US.

MAYBE WE DON'T NEED TO USE WHITE ARROWS...

...TO PUT A STOP TO METROPOLIMAN AND *GIRL A*. RED ARROWS WOULD ALSO WORK.

IN THAT CASE...

...IF ONE OF METRO-POLIMAN'S COMPANIONS HITS MIRAI WITH A RED ARROW AT THAT POINT, EVERYTHING WILL FLIP AGAINST US.

METROPOLIMAN ALREADY HAS TWO SETS OF WINGS AND ARROWS.

BASED ON THE EVENTS AT THE STADIUM, HE IS CAPABLE OF ANYTHING. I AGREE THAT IF WE HAVE THE OPPORTUNITY, WE OUGHT TO KILL HIM.

...

I UNDER-STAND WHAT YOU'RE SAYING.
BUT MY MIND CAN'T PROCESS IT.

I DON'T KNOW...
...IF THAT MAKES IT *RIGHT* TO KILL SOMEONE ...

IF YOU DON'T KILL HIM, HE'LL KILL YOU.
DON'T YOU SEE THAT?
...

I'D RATHER BE LIED TO THAN BE A LIAR. I'D RATHER BE BULLIED THAN BE A BULLY.
I'D RATHER BE MURDERED... THAN BE A MURDERER.

I LIVED BY THAT CREED UNTIL I EVENTUALLY ATTEMPTED SUICIDE.
I BELIEVED THAT NO MATTER WHAT, I MUST NEVER HATE ANOTHER PERSON...

...
WHOA... ARE YOU SERI-OUS?
...

THAT MIGHT BE THE PROPER WAY FOR A SAINT TO LIVE, BUT EVEN A LITTLE KID KNOWS YOU CAN'T SURVIVE THE REAL WORLD WITH THAT MIND-SET!
I UNDER-STAND THAT... AND HOW THAT LED TO MY SUICIDE ATTEMPT...
...AND THAT THE STAKES ARE TOO HIGH TO STICK TO THAT NOW. I UNDERSTAND THE LOGIC BEHIND ALL OF IT.
BUT...

BUT THAT'S THE BEST PART ABOUT YOU, MIRAI.
IN MY OPINION.
...
...
THINK OF IT THIS WAY THEN.
LET'S SAY THAT I...
NO, THAT MS. HANAKAGO HERE IS ABOUT TO BE KILLED BY METROPOLIMAN.
AND YOU ARE IN A POSITION TO HIT METROPOLIMAN FIRST WITHOUT HIM NOTICING.

YOU CAN ONLY USE ONE ARROW.
DO YOU USE RED OR WHITE?

USE A RED ARROW ...
...OR A WHITE ARROW ...?

BA-BUMP

WHUP
BA-BMP
RED ...
...OR WHITE ...
BA-BMP
IF HE'S LET HIS COMPANION HIT HIM WITH A RED ARROW...
WHITE ...
WHITE ...?!
...THEN MY RED WON'T WORK ON METROPOLIMAN...
BOTH SAKI AND I WILL DIE!
GRRRG

AAAAAH!!

KW

NO-OO-OO!!
DON'T DO IT!!

WHUP

KAKE-HASHI!
HUFF !!
HEY! WHAT'S WRONG ?!
HUFF !!
HUFF !!
TALK TO US!
HUFF !!
HUFF!
HUFF!
HUFF!
...
WHITE ...

USING WHITE ...
USING A WHITE ARROW TO KILL HIM IS...
...

OKAY, WE'LL LEAVE IT AT THAT FOR TODAY.
PHEW.

BUT STILL, THE CHOICE WILL COME SOMEDAY...

I'LL BRING BARET ALONG TOMORROW, AND WE CAN HAVE A STUDY AND STRATEGY SESSION.
IF THEY'RE TRYING TO LURE GOD CANDIDATES INTO THE OPEN, THEY'LL SEND OUT A CLEAR SIGNAL.

THAT'S RIGHT. AND UNTIL THEN, WE SHOULDN'T ACT RECK-LESSLY.

KAKE-HASHI...

GOING BACK TO THAT HYPOTHETICAL ...
IF I AM THE ONE ABOUT TO BE KILLED, YOU CAN USE RED.
...

KSHUNK
I HAVE A HARD TIME IMAGINING METROPOLIMAN WOULD LET EVEN HIS COMPANION USE A RED ARROW ON HIMSELF.
BE-SIDES ...
MR. MUKAIDO ...

I'M SORRY ...

BUT I WANT YOU TO LIVE AS LONG AS YOU POSSIBLY CAN...

...

GEEZ, KID.

YOU'RE GONNA MAKE ME CRY.

SEE YOU TOMOR-ROW.

ZWIP

FWUF...
FWUF...
YOU REALLY THINK WE CAN REEL THEM IN WITH *THIS*?

PERHAPS THERE ARE ONE OR TWO SOFTHEARTED FOOLS AMONG THE REMAINING CANDIDATES.
IF NO ONE SHOWS UP, THAT'S FINE TOO. MINAMIKAWA'S DREAM FOR ALL UGLY GIRLS TO DISAPPEAR WILL COME TRUE.

THE NEXT DAY

六階堂
MUKAIDO

DADDY, YOU HAVE SO MANY PILLS!

CLINK

CLINK

HERE'S YOUR WATER!

THANK YOU, NANAKA.

...

ARE YOU SURE IT'S HEALTHY FOR YOU TO BE TAKING SO MANY TRIPS OUT, NANATO?
IT'S A SIGN OF MY GOOD HEALTH.

BVV
BVV
BVV
!
...
NEWS ALWAYS COMES VIA THE PHONE FIRST.

BIP
BODY FOUND ATOP GRAND TOWER
THIS JUST IN.

BREAK
BODY FOUND ATOP GRAND TOWER
A DEAD BODY HAS BEEN FOUND ATOP THE PROMONTORY PLATFORM AT THE VERY TOP OF GRAND TOWER.
IT WAS IDENTIFIED AS HIKARI YAISHI, AGE 14, WHO WAS REPORTED MISSING LAST NIGHT...

REAL VISIBLE SPOT TO PLACE A BODY... OR NOT VISIBLE, I GUESS...
IN EITHER CASE, OBVIOUSLY DONE WITH WINGS.
BODY FOUND ATOP GRAND TOWER
SHE WAS IN SHIBUYA WITH FOUR FRIENDS AS RECENTLY AS ONE O'CLOCK YESTERDAY AFTERNOON...
...AND BY 1:30, WAS NOT RESPONDING TO CONTACT ATTEMPTS, ACCORDING TO STATEMENTS.
AND GIRL A'S ESCAPE WAS AROUND MIDDAY YESTERDAY. THAT WAS FAST...

A YOUNG TEEN GIRL, HANGING OUT IN SHIBUYA...

WAIT A SECOND...
!

NO... IT COULDN'T BE.
UNLESS-
KTHUMP
I'M HEADING OUT!
DSH DSH
NANATO?
HE REALLY IS FEELING BETTER...
WHUP
LET'S GO, BARET!
SHHP
OKAY.
GSH
GUESS I SHOULD TAKE THIS, JUST IN CASE.

THPPA THPPA

THPPA

HIKARI'S CAROTID ARTERY AND WRISTS WERE SEVERED WITH A SHARP BLADE...

THPPA

THPPA

CAROTID ARTERY AND WRISTS...

THE SAME METHODS AS *GIRL A'S* PAST THREE MURDERS.

TAP TAP TAP TAP TAP TAP
OH, THAT'S MUKAIDO.
SIX TAPS AT THE WINDOW. IT'S SO STUPID.
Just because his name has the kanji for "six"...

BAWHUMP
THIS IS MY ANGEL, BARET.
IT IS A PLEASURE TO MEET YOU.
FWUF...
I'M NASSE! NICE TO MEET YOU, BARET!
I AM REVEL.
TSK ...
HELLO ...

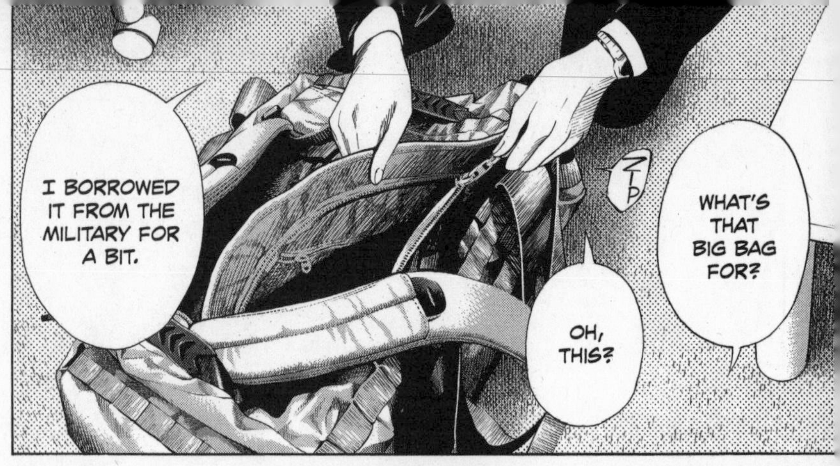

JUST AN ASSORTMENT OF SUPPLIES ...

HUH?

THIS MIGHT NOT MATCH A WHITE ARROW THAT CAN PIERCE BULLETPROOF GLASS AND NEVER MISS...
...BUT IT SHOULD COME IN HANDY.
CHK

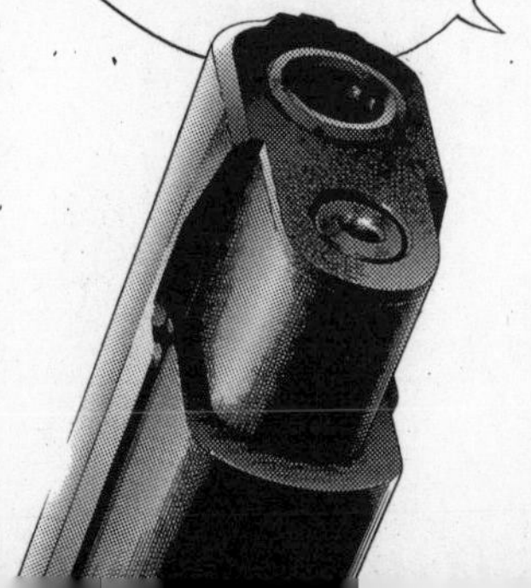
ON THE OTHER HAND, IT FEELS LIKE IT SHOULD BE AGAINST THE RULES TO USE THIS IN A COMPETITION TO DECIDE GOD WITH WINGS AND ARROWS.

NOT TRUE.
USING HUMAN CREATIONS TO KILL A GOD CANDIDATE DOES NOT DISQUALIFY ONE FROM BEING GOD.

WHOA, REALLY?
REALLY.
THAT'LL MAKE THEM EVEN MORE USEFUL.
I DIDN'T GIVE A CRAP ABOUT THE RULES, BUT...
...NOW YOU CAN HAVE THEM TOO.
CHK
AH... I...
...

IS THIS A SICK JOKE?!

DO I LOOK LIKE I'M JOKING?

I'M ABSOLUTELY SERIOUS.

THIS IS A CRIME! YOU'LL BE ARRESTED IN NO TIME!

YOU REALLY HAVE A KNACK FOR SAYING STUFF THAT EVEN A LITTLE KID KNOWS. SAVE YOUR BREATH.

WHITE ARROWS LEAVE NO WOUNDS, AND THUS NO PROOF-- THEY TRULY ARE GIFTS FROM AN ANGEL.
BUT THAT MEANS THAT GUNS ARE QUITE EFFECTIVE AGAINST THOSE WHO ASSUME KILLING MEANS USING WHITE ARROWS. WE MIGHT HAVE BEEN ABLE TO KILL HIM WITH THESE AT THE STADIUM.

I'M SAYING, DO YOU WANT YOUR CHILDREN TO GROW UP WITH A MURDERER FOR A FATHER?

THAT ONE *DOESN'T* MAKE ME CRY.
...
LISTEN... NO MATTER WHO STOPS METROPOLIMAN, OR HOW...
...THE ONE WHO DOES ...
SHHK
...WILL BE A HERO ONCE THE ENTIRE TRUTH IS LAID BARE.
KLCH
I'M NOT SAYING THIS BECAUSE I WANT TO BE A HERO.
SHINK

I JUST DON'T WANT TO BE THE FATHER WHO ACHIEVED NOTHING ...
THE FATHER WHO DIDN'T EVEN *TRY* FOR THE SAKE OF HIS CHILDREN.

I GOT THE OPPORTUNITY TO BE A CANDIDATE.
I'M GOING TO TAKE THAT RESPONSIBILITY AND DO EVERYTHING I POSSIBLY CAN WITH IT.

THE RESPONSIBILITY OF A CANDIDATE...
WE OUGHT TO HURRY.
THE IDEA THAT *GIRL A* COULD KILL UP TO 14 PEOPLE WITH RED ARROWS IN 33 DAYS...
...WAS INCORRECT.
?!
BUT THE RED ARROWS CAN ONLY PIERCE UP TO 14 TARGETS.
THAT'S ONLY TECHNICALLY TRUE.
EXPLAIN, BARET.
OKAY.

PLIP
WHEN A HUMAN PIERCED BY A RED ARROW DIES, THE ARROW RETURNS TO THE HAND OF THE ONE WHO USED IT.
EVEN IF ALL 14 ARROWS ARE USED, IF THE 14 VICTIMS DIE, THE ARROWS WILL RETURN AND CAN BE USED AGAIN.
SO AS LONG AS THE USER KILLS THE VICTIMS, THE NUMBER OF ARROWS AT THEIR DISPOSAL IS INFINITE.
...
WOW, BARET'S EXPLANATION WAS REALLY GOOD.
RIGHT? RIGHT?
ER, I SUPPOSE ...
I didn't know that.

I PROCURED A NUMBER OF OTHER THINGS.
BUT WE DON'T HAVE TIME. WE'VE GOT TO MOVE INTO ACTION RIGHT AWAY.
!

DON'T WORRY. I'M NOT TELLING YOU TO KILL ANYONE. JUST HIT METROPOLIMAN WITH A RED ARROW.
ZIP
...!

WELL? ARE YOU COMING?
YES, OF COURSE!

THE NUMBER OF VICTIMS INCREASES WITH EVERY PASSING MINUTE.
WE NEED TO WRAP THIS UP AS QUICKLY AS WE CAN!
FWUP

DRIP
DRIP
DRIP

HUFF!
HUFF!

IT FEELS SO GOOD. I THINK I'M GONNA EXPLODE.
SHIVER

TIME TO GO PICK THE NEXT FRUIT.
GLORP
SHIBUYA, HERE I COME!
MEW!
OH!
FORGOT TO PUT CLOTHES ON.
Mistakerin!

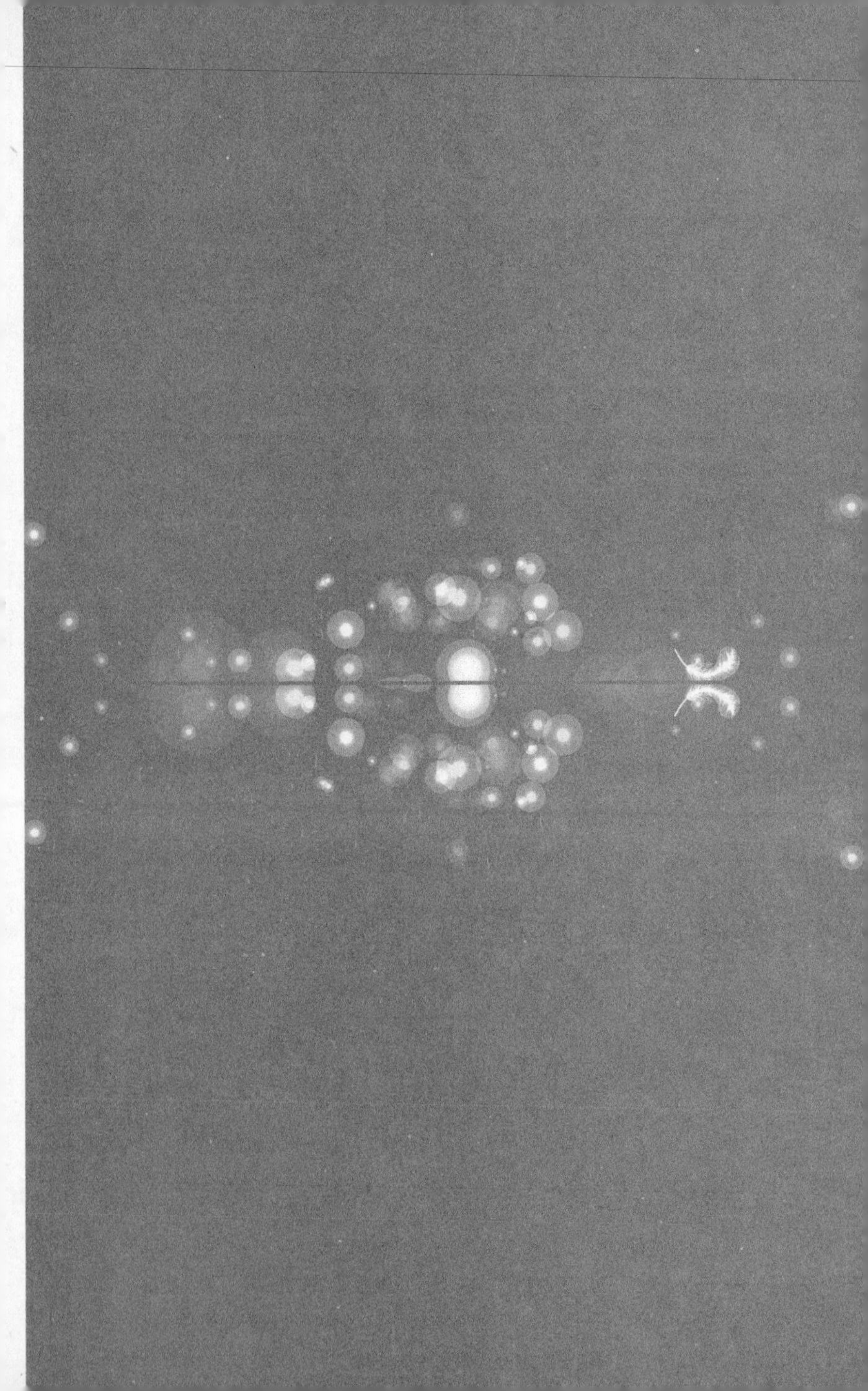

#9 Tower of Nightmares

MASTER POLIMAAAN!

SHE'S STARTING TO SMELL!

I WANNA DUMP THE BODY ALREADY.

HOW DOES YOUR DUMPING SPOT LOOK NOW?

IT'S FINE! NOBODY'S THERE.

NOBODY'S THERE...?

OF COURSE NOBODY'S UP AT A PLACE LIKE THIS.

UGHHH, I CAN'T TAKE IT!
WUP

THEN TAKE A PICTURE THAT MAKES THE LOCATION CLEAR AND SPREAD IT ON THE NET.
KLICK
WHOA! THAT SOUNDS CRAZY.
OKAY, I CAN DO THAT! ♡
KLICK
KLICK

...
BEEP

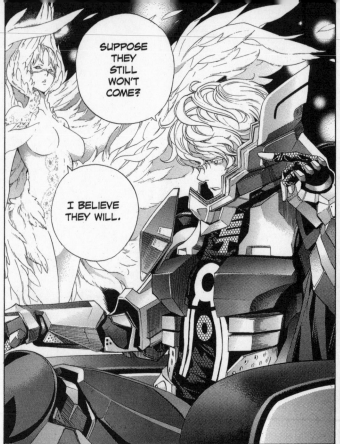

SUPPOSE THEY STILL WON'T COME?
I BELIEVE THEY WILL.

HMPH.

IF IT DOESN'T WORK, WE'LL NEED SOME MUCH BIGGER FIREWORKS.

FWAP
LISTEN UP. GIRL A'S THREE VICTIMS FROM TWO YEARS AGO WERE IN THEIR SCHOOL UNIFORMS.
THE PLACES THEY VANISHED FROM ARE HARAJUKU, SHIBUYA AND HARAJUKU, IN THAT ORDER.

THE VICTIM ON TOP OF GRAND TOWER YESTERDAY WAS IN HER UNIFORM, AND VANISHED FROM SHIBUYA.
WHICH MEANS THAT *GIRL A* WILL STRIKE NEXT IN HARAJUKU!

!

DING-DONG!
BREAKING NEWS
A NEWS UPDATE!
AH.

BREAKING NEWS
ANOTHER YOUNG WOMAN'S BODY FOUND ATOP GRAND TOWER
!

WE BRING YOU THIS BREAKING NEWS.
UPLOADED IMAGE
BREAKING
ANOTHER YOUNG WOMAN'S BODY FOUND ATOP GRAND TOWER
FOLLOWING THE DISCOVERY OF THE BODY OF HIKARI YAISHI, AGE 14 YESTERDAY, A PICTURE OF A NEW VICTIM ATOP GRAND TOWER WAS UPLOADED ONTO SOCIAL MEDIA...

ON SOCIAL MEDIA?

WHAT?!
...

DAMN!
WHAP

TO STOP *GIRL A*, I ASSUMED WE SHOULD SEARCH IN SHIBUYA OR HARAJUKU.
AND I ALSO ASSUMED THAT ***THEY*** WOULD USE THAT TO GO AFTER US...

BUT THEY WENT STRAIGHT FOR GRAND TOWER FROM THE START.

THIS ISN'T A BATTLE OF WITS.
WE SHOULD THINK OF IT MUCH MORE SIMPLY...

JUST BEING ABLE TO GET ATOP GRAND TOWER MEANS YOU'RE A GOD CANDIDATE!
!

ANOTHER YOUNG WOMAN'S BODY FOUND ATOP GRAND TOWER
I SEE.
IN THE STADIUM, WE WERE ABLE TO HIDE IN THE CROWD TO WATCH...
BUT THERE'S NO HIDING UP THERE.
HE WANTS TO FIGHT OUT IN THE OPEN, AT THE TOP OF THE TOWER.
!

BUT WE CAN'T JUST WAIT FOR THE NEXT BODY TO SHOW UP. WE NEED TO STAKE OUT SHIBUYA OR HARAJUKU...
RIGHT... AT THIS RATE, THERE'S A DEATH A DAY. THAT'S AT LEAST 33 BODIES IN 33 DAYS.

THIRTY-THREE VICTIMS...
HANG ON.

IT SOUNDS LIKE *GIRL A* IS STILL HOVERING OVER GRAND TOWER.

?!

PEOPLE ARE ALL TALKING ABOUT "MISURIN FLYING."

THERE'S TONS OF PICTURES AND VIDEOS...

Mi_su_ri_n
It's Misurin☆

Misurin Maniac (u_u)
Whoa! Misurin's flying

Minmin
Misurin's flying above the tow

missmisslin @missmisslin
(((o(*ﾟ▽ﾟ*)o))) Misurin! Misurin!

Failed to Sleep
Oh crap!! Misurin's flying over Grand Tower ☆

MRMR
MURMUR
MURMUR
LOOK, UP THERE!
WHAT, REALLY ?!
PEOPLE, PLEASE!
THE TOWER IS TEMPORARILY SHUT DOWN! WE NEED YOU TO...
MRMR
MRMR
MISURIN IS UP THERE ...
WHOOOOO
...
WHAT... IS GOING ON HERE ...?

WHOOSH

WHO... ARE YOU ...?
YAWN!
MMMM.

OH NOOO! I REALLY TRIPPED OUT THERE!
I was napping with Poliman! ♡
WHAT A MISTAKERIN !!
KNOCK IT OFF.
SORRY, MASTER POLIMAN!
!
ONE, TWO, THREE ...
SIX IN ALL...
WELL, IT'S A WASTE, BUT...
OH WELL!
?!
HERE WE GO.
SWING...

GRIN
MISU-
RIIIN
FLASH
!!
SHUM

MISURIIIIN…
ZWOOP
SHAK
ATTACK!
TWINNG

FWUP
MISU-RIN GAL-AXY!!
SHAK
MISU-RIN STAR-LIGHT!!
MISU-RIN EXCEL-LENT!!
THD THD THD THD THD
MPD

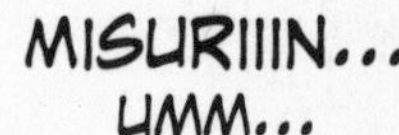
MISURIIIN... UMM...

HFF
HFF

ROLLING ... THUNDER?
SHAK

GRIN

PHEW——!

OKAY, I'VE PIERCED YOU ALL. TAKE THE BODY AND GO BACK DOWN.

AND MAKE SURE THAT NO ONE ELSE CAN COME UP HERE. ♡

YES, OF COURSE!
I'M JUST HAPPY TO HAVE MET YOU IN PERSON!
CAN YOU GIVE ME AN AUTOGRAPH LATER...?
KWIIIIIII
ZSH
WHAT... THE HELL... ARE YOU SAYING?!
DON'T LEAVE THIS SPOT...
HUH? MISURIN ASKED US TO DO IT.
IF ANYONE'S BEING WEIRD, IT'S YOU, MR. HAYASHI.
DON'T BE... IDIOTS...
HAVE YOU NO PRIDE AS POLICEMEN?!
KWIII

I MIGHT... LOVE... MISURIN...

...BUT SHE'S A... MURDERER ...

KWIIII

SO WHAT?

FORGET IT. LET'S JUST GO.

WHOA!

NICE WORK, GRAMPS! YOU'RE FIGHTING BACK AGAINST THE RED ARROW!
TALK ABOUT DEDICATING YOUR LIFE TO YOUR JOB! WHAT IS THAT, LIKE 36 YEARS ON THE JOB?! HILARIOUS!

BUT YOU'RE INTERFERING WITH ME, SO TAKE HIM AWAY. ♡

YES, MISURIN! ♡

DAMN YOUUU!!

UGH...

SNAG

GCHA

NK

THERE'S NO ONE LEFT, MASTER POLIMAN.
WHOOSH
THEN DO AS I SAID.
OKAAAAAY.
LET'S GO, KAKEHASHI!

GIRL A ISN'T ACTING UNDER HER OWN WILL.
IT'S METRO-POLIMAN.
DSHH
SINCE THE BODY WAS DUMPED THERE YESTERDAY, HE'S BEEN HOPING THAT A GOD CANDIDATE WOULD COME.
SO HE HAS GIRL A SIT OVER THE TOWER, AND WHEN A CANDIDATE SHOWS UP, HITS THEM WITH A WHITE ARROW.

...

WHICH MEANS ...

FIRST, I'LL ACT AS BAIT AND FACE OFF AGAINST *GIRL A.*
WHEN METROPOLIMAN COMES TO KILL ME, YOU HIT HIM WITH THE ARROW.

THIS IS ***ALSO*** THE PERFECT CHANCE TO HIT METROPOLIMAN WITH A RED ARROW!
!
I CAN'T USE ANY ARROWS RIGHT NOW, REMEMBER.
!

ALL RIGHT.

OR YOU CAN USE WHITE...

!

OR RED. RED IS FINE.
RIGHT, BARET?
YES.

IF A PERSON WITH RED ARROWS IS HIT BY A RED ARROW, IT IS POSSIBLE TO COMMAND THEM TO HIT YOU WITH ONE OF THOSE ARROWS.

BUT THAT WILL NULLIFY THE ORIGINAL ARROW AND ACTIVATE THE NEWER ONE, EFFECTIVELY REVERSING YOUR POSITIONS.

OHHHH!!
You know everything, don't you!
GRKK...
WHICH MEANS IT SEEMS VERY UNLIKELY THAT HE IS DOING THAT.

CHK
IF WE HIT HIM WITH RED, WE CAN HANDLE EVERYTHING ELSE, INCLUDING *GIRL A.*
I WAS THINKING OF HAVING EITHER KAKEHASHI OR HANAKAGO PIERCE ME WITH AN ARROW FIRST, TO ENSURE THAT I DIDN'T GET HIT WITH A RED ARROW FROM THE CROWDS IN SHIBUYA OR HARAJUKU...
...BUT I APPRECIATE THAT WE'RE GOING TO THAT TOWER INSTEAD, WHERE THE VISIBILITY IS GOOD.
SHNK
FWUP
IT'S A DIRECT CONFRONTATION!

YES, APPEARANCE-WISE, IT WOULD SUIT YOU BEST, HANAKAGO, BUT WE'RE NOT LOOKING FOR REALISM.

METROPOLIMAN'S JUST LOOKING FOR GOD CANDIDATES TO SHOW UP.

AND I DON'T WANT TO MAKE YOU BAIT, SINCE YOU DON'T HAVE WINGS.

Is he serious ...?

SHWIP

CHANGE INTO THAT. I PUT IT TOGETHER FOR YOU.
FWUMP
SHUM
I BORROWED MY OUTFIT FROM THE JAPAN SELF-DEFENSE FORCES.
KLAK
ZIP

KLAK
PHEW...
THAT'S VERY THICK ARMOR...
IT LOOKS HEAVY...
ARE YOU SURE YOU'LL BE ABLE TO WEAR IT AROUND?
YEAH. IT'S HEAVY FOR A SICK MAN TO CARRY...
...BUT WEIGHT DOESN'T AFFECT THE FLIGHT SPEED OF THE WINGS.
RIGHT, BARET?
YES.
CREAK
IT IS FINE, AS LONG AS THE WEARER CAN SUPPORT IT WITH HIS OWN STRENGTH. BUT YOU CAN ONLY CARRY ONE OTHER PERSON.

HOW IS THE SIZE, KAKEHASHI?
OOH.
LOOKS PERFECT TO ME.

...
THAT'S MOTORSPORTS WEAR DEVELOPED BY MY COMPANY.
GRK...
IT'S A NEW MATERIAL MADE FROM LEATHER AND ARAMID FIBERS...
IT'S LIGHT, FRICTION AND SHOCK RESISTANT, DOESN'T PUNCTURE EASILY, AND BOTH STRETCHABLE AND BREATHABLE.
WITH THE DUST MASK AND HOOD, YOU CAN HIDE YOUR FACE TOO.

IT WAS TOO EXPENSIVE TO MASS-PRODUCE...
...BUT I'M GLAD IT CAME IN HANDY HERE.
YOU LOOK LIKE A SUPER-HERO, MIRAI!
HE DOES...
...
BARET AND NASSE, COME WITH US.
REVEL AND HANAKAGO, YOU STAY HERE.
THERE'S NO CHANCE THEY'LL ATTACK HERE. CONTACT US IF ANYTHING HAPPENS.
I'M JUST GOING TO SAY ONE THING, KAKEHASHI.
SHHK
OKAY.

THERE'S ANOTHER REASON I SAID I "APPRECIATED" THAT HE WANTS A CONFRONTATION ATOP THE TOWER.
I HAVE A FAMILY. IF WE WERE GOING TO PLACE A RED ARROW IN ME AS A SAFEGUARD IN SHIBUYA AND HARAJUKU, I WAS GOING TO HAVE YOU DO IT, NOT HANAKAGO.

IF THAT HAPPENED, I WOULDN'T BE ABLE TO DISOBEY YOUR ORDERS.

I WOULDN'T BE ABLE TO KILL.

W-WHAT ...
... DO YOU MEAN BY THAT ...?

I'M TALKING HYPOTHETICALLY.
SHK
LET'S SAY THAT METROPOLIMAN DOESN'T SHOW UP...
CHAK

THEN I'LL KILL *GIRL A.*

SHE'S AN UNCONTROL-LABLE MONSTER. SHE'S GOT HER OWN WINGS AND SHE'S ALREADY CONTROLLED BY A RED ARROW.

I NEED TO KILL HER.

DO YOU REALLY THINK THEY CAN BE CAPTURED?

...

ALL RIGHT.

IF SHE CAN'T SEE US, SHE CAN'T SHOOT AN ARROW. RIGHT, BARET?
BUT AT THE VERY LEAST, I'LL TAKE OUT HER EYES.
YEAH, I KNEW THAT TOO. IF YOU CAN'T SEE THE TARGET, YOUR ARROW WON'T STRIKE TRUE.
IF WE LET HER ESCAPE, SHE'LL MURDER MORE INNOCENT GIRLS.
IF ANYONE DESERVES THE KNIFE, IT'S THE SERIAL KILLER!
YES.
YOU'RE NOT GOING TO TELL ME YOU DISAGREE WITH *THAT*.
...

JUST PROMISE ME THAT I'LL GET TO FINISH OFF METROPOLIMAN WHILE I STILL LIVE.
HMPH
SHH...
KAKEHASHI.
TUG

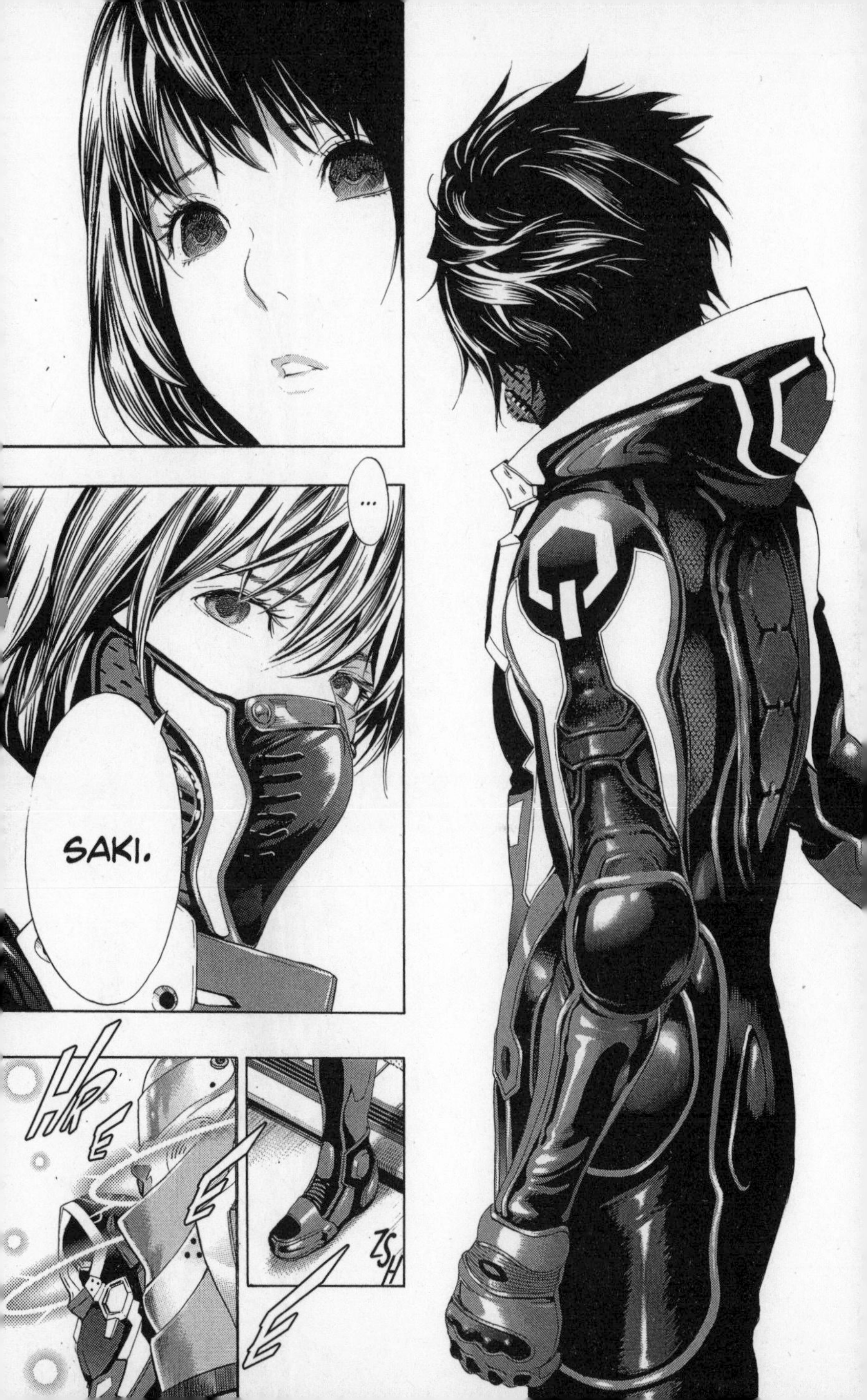
...
SAKI.
ZSH
HREEE

IF METROPOLIMAN DOESN'T SHOW UP...
...MR. MUKAIDO WILL KILL GIRL A.
NO...
KILLING SOMEONE IS...
GRK

PLEASE COME...
...METRO-POLIMAN!
SO I CAN HIT YOU...
...WITH MY RED ARROW!

TAP TAP
TAP
awason
Kawaii Ribbon Barrette
Price: ¥1,380 In stock.
Place in Cart
Buy Now
TAP
WHAT DO YOU THINK YOU'RE DOING?

WHOOOOO
ROLL...
ONLINE SHOPPING.
HERE WE GO.

BA-BUMP

WHOOO
BA-BUMP
BA-BUMP
WHOOOO
BA-BUMP

I WAS LOOKING FOR A CUTE RIBBON.
I'M NOT TALKING ABOUT THAT.
I MEAN, WHY ARE YOU HERE?
I'M WAITING FOR MASTER POLIMAN.

IS HE COMING?
...

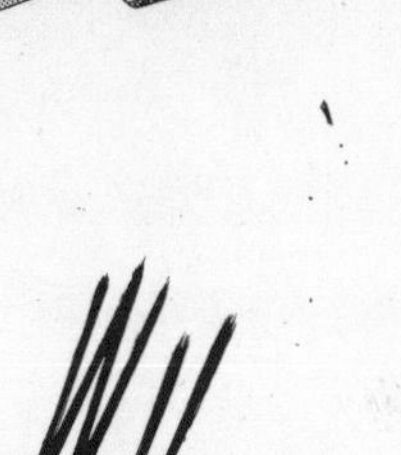
HEY...
WHY DIDN'T YOU SHOOT ME BEFORE I NOTICED YOU?
NOW THAT I'VE SEEN YOU, I CAN JUST FLY AWAY TO SAFETY.
WHOOSH

AND WHY DIDN'T *YOU* USE YOUR RED ARROWS?

HEE HEE...

HE TOLD ME THAT IF SOMEONE FLEW UP HERE...
C'MON.
SO DON'T JUST STAND AT THE EDGE THERE.
COME CLOSER ...

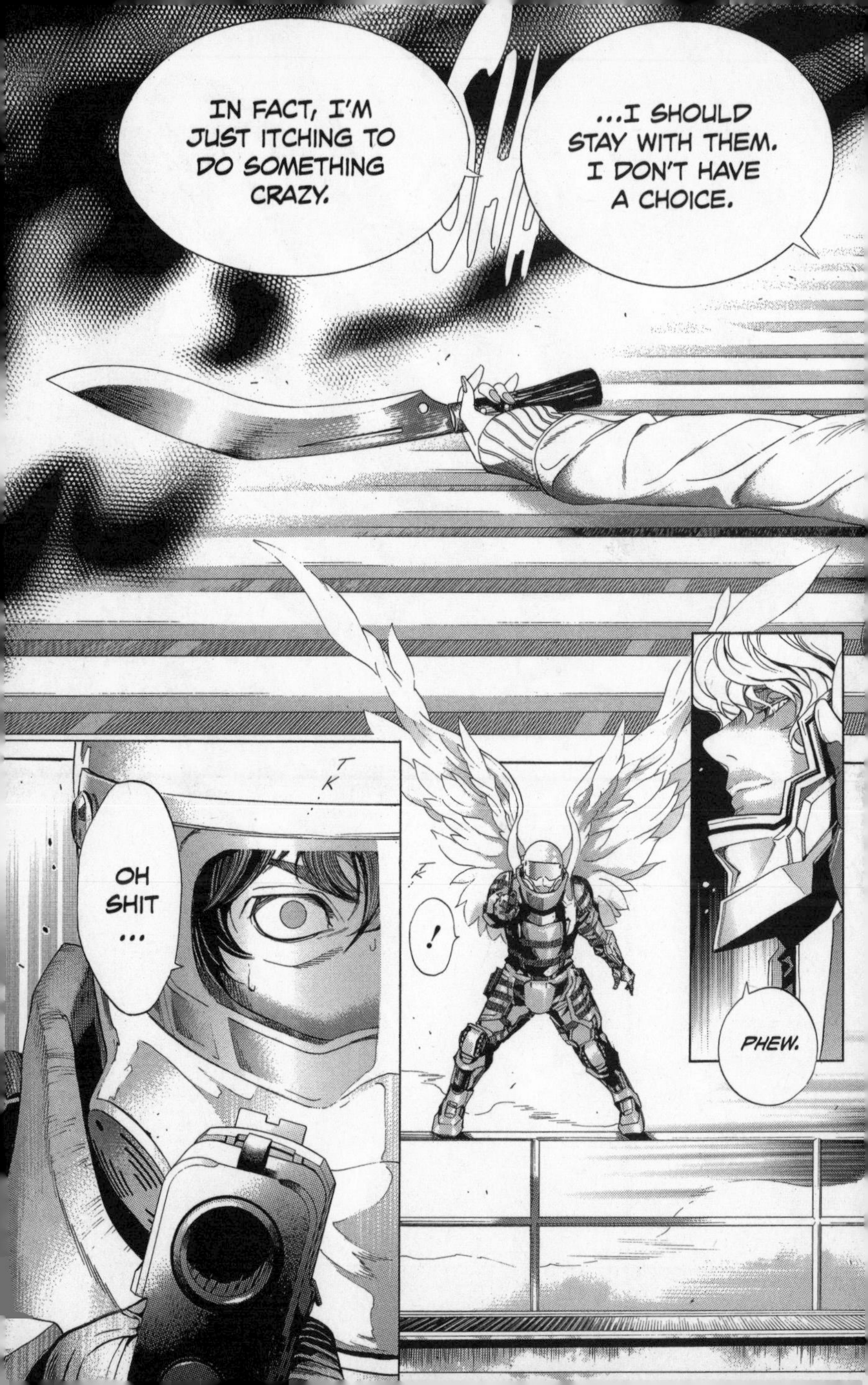
...I SHOULD STAY WITH THEM. I DON'T HAVE A CHOICE.
IN FACT, I'M JUST ITCHING TO DO SOMETHING CRAZY.
PHEW.
TK
!
TK
OH SHIT ...

METROPOLIMAN WASN'T COMING WITH A WHITE ARROW...?

WHA...

WHAT'S...
...HAPPENING...?

HUH ...?

MR. MUKAIDO!!
DA
DA
DA
DOOM
VWOOM
NO...
NO...

BADOOM
BRRRRRRR
VMMMM
FSH
FSH
FSH
HUFF!!
HUFF!!
FSH
OH CRAP!!
AAAAH!!
A TERRORIST BOMBING?!

WHUP
HUFF!!
HUFF!!

MR. MUKAI-DO!
BSST
BSST

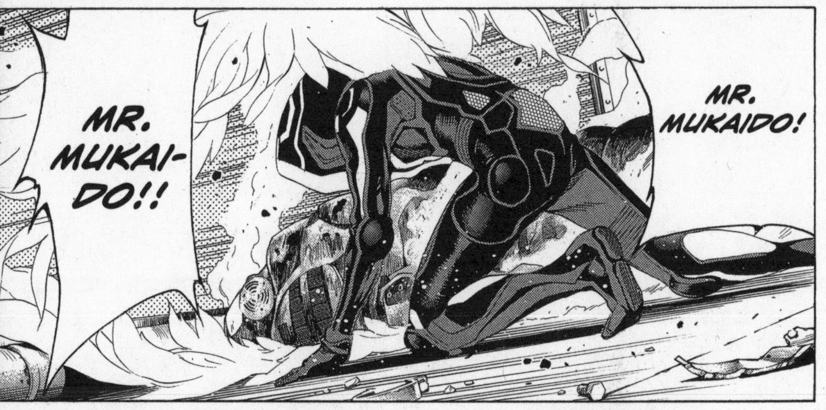
MR. MUKAIDO!
MR. MUKAI-DO!!

PLEASE ... YOU CAN'T DIE!
MR. MU-KAI-DO !!

NO... NO, DON'T DIE...
TUG
TUG

I'M SICK OF PEOPLE DYING!!
MR. MUKAI-DO...

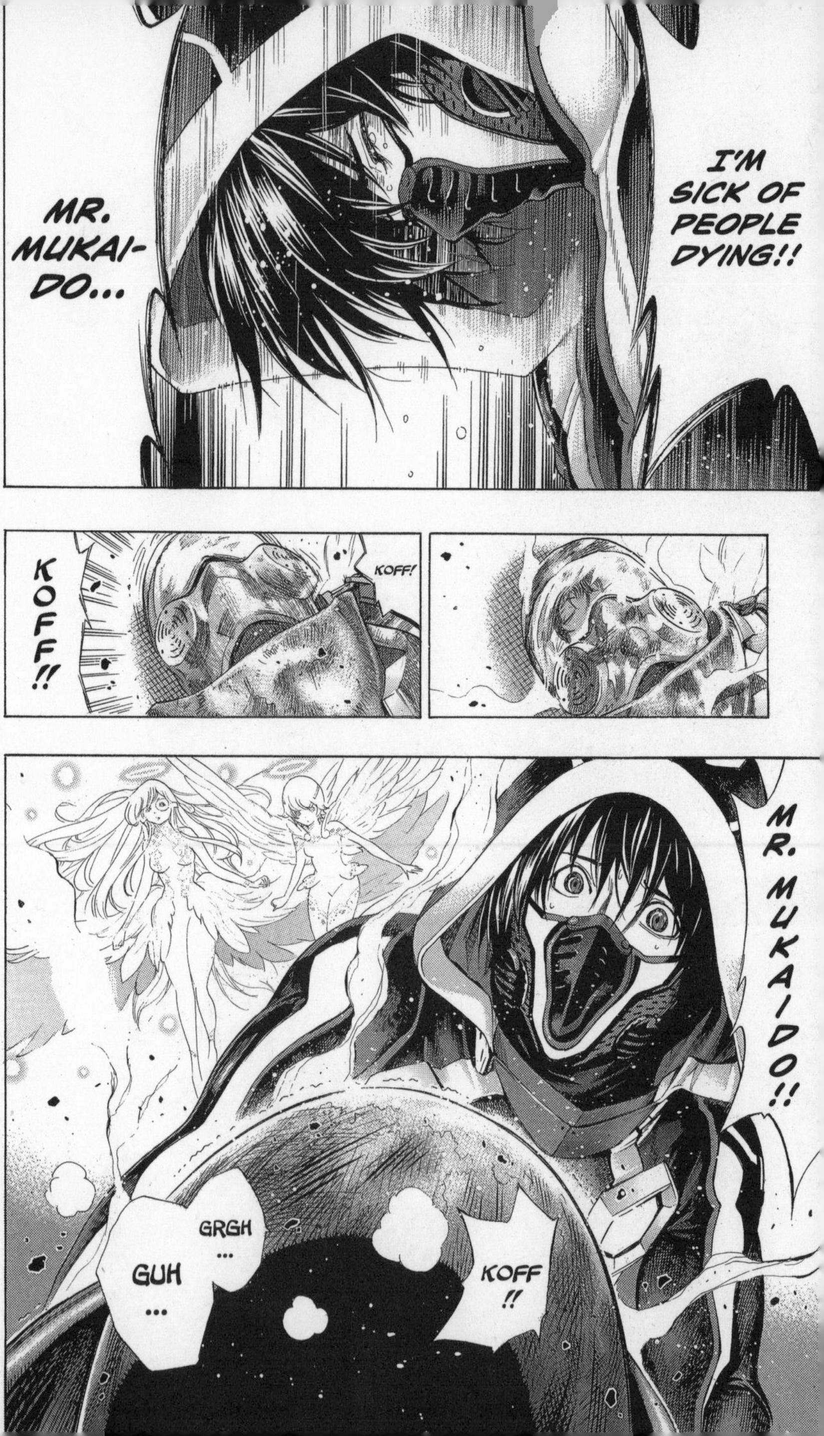

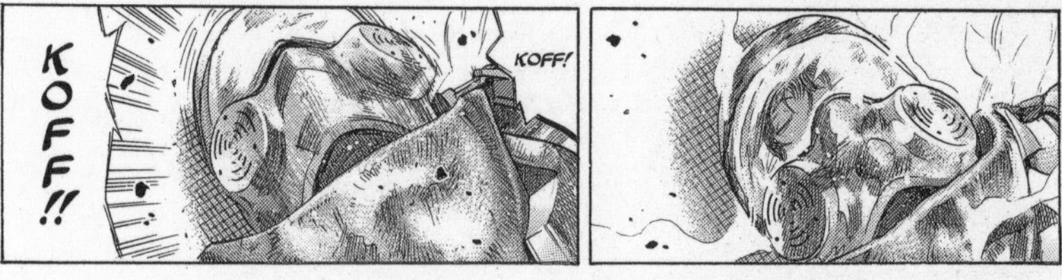
KOFF!
KOFF!!

MR. MUKAIDO!!

KOFF!!

GRGH...

GUH...

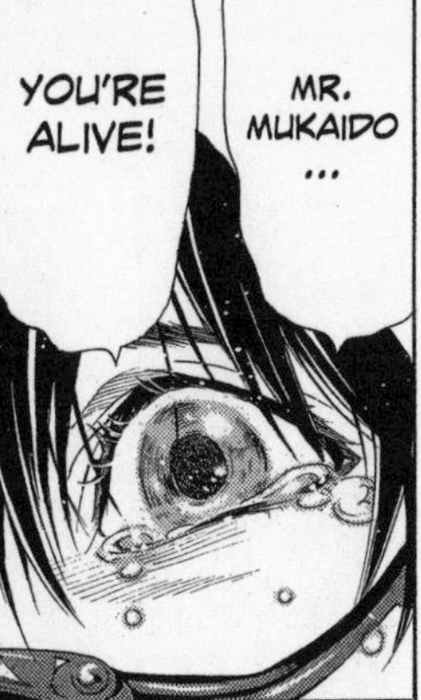
MR. MUKAIDO ...
YOU'RE ALIVE!

HE MADE IT!
YES. OF COURSE, WE COULD TELL THAT IMMEDIATELY.

IS THAT... YOU, KAKE-HASHI ...?
HUFF!
HUFF!

RMB

RMB
RMB
GLAD I PICKED THE ANTI-EXPLOSIVE SUIT, JUST IN CASE...
THE KIND THAT BOMB SQUADS WEAR...
HUFF!
HUFF!
HUFF!
RMB

I CON-SIDERED THIS AN OUTSIDE POSSIBILITY, BUT I DIDN'T THINK HE'D DO IT ON THIS SCALE...

HE WON'T LIMIT HIS KILLING TO THE WHITE ARROWS NOW.
...

I GUESS I WAS A SPLIT-SECOND TOO LATE TO FLY...

IN ANY CASE, I'D BE DEAD IF YOU WEREN'T HERE...

RMB
I'M GLAD.
RMB

YOU DON'T WANT TO SEE ANY MORE PEOPLE DIE.
THAT'S WHAT YOU SAID.

...
YES.

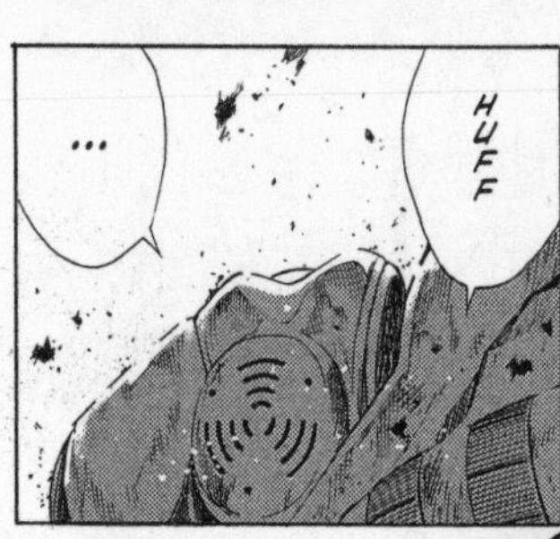
HUFF
...

SO GIRL A... DIED IN THE BLAST.

I AGREE... I DON'T WANT TO SEE PEOPLE DIE...

GRRGGR
RGG
RG
THE SHOW'S ABOUT TO BEGIN.
BUT IT LOOKS LIKE...
...WE HAVE NO TIME TO GET SENTIMENTAL.
RG
GRG
GR
HE'S HERE.

R
RR
R
WHAT'S WITH THAT COSTUME?
R
G

TO BE CONTINUED...

Tsugumi Ohba

Born in Tokyo, Tsugumi Ohba is the author of the hit series *Death Note* and *Bakuman。*.

Takeshi Obata

Takeshi Obata was born in 1969 in Niigata, Japan, and first achieved international recognition as the artist of the wildly popular *Shonen Jump* title *Hikaru no Go*, which won the 2003 Tezuka Osamu Cultural Prize: Shinsei "New Hope" Award and the 2000 Shogakukan Manga Award. He went on to illustrate the smash hit *Death Note* as well as the hugely successful manga *Bakuman。* and *All You Need Is Kill*.